HURTING
AND
HEALING

HURTING AND HEALING

GLORIA WADE

vega

A catalogue record for this book is available from the
British Library.

ISBN 1-84333-095-4
Printed by CPD Wales, Ebbw Vale

© Vega 2001

A member of the Chrysalis Group plc

Published in 2001 by
Vega
8-10 Blenheim Court
Brewery Road
London N7 9NY

Visit our Website at www.chrysalisbooks.co.uk

If you or someone close to you has suffered from abuse this is a book that could change your life. If you are a professional working in this difficult and painful area, or just want to understand it better it will also be a valuable guide.

Gloria Wade writes with compassion about the suffering abuse causes, but her approach is extremely positive about the potential within each of us for healing. She sweeps away the false shame, secrecy and confusion that keeps people in a victim mentality. The exercises she suggests are based on the hundreds of hours of workshops she has conducted and they are safe and practical.

I wish this book could have been present years ago when services like my own were struggling with the increasing numbers of children and adults coming forward for help and acknowledging abuse. At that time we had to face our own lack of therapeutic skills in this very special field and work to protect and heal in an often uncomprehending world.

This book is the most balanced approach I have come across and should be required reading for doctors, nurses, social workers, the police, journalists, lawyers, judges and the general public, as well as those who have direct experience of abuse.

Elinor Kapp

MB. BS. DPM. FRC Psych.
(Consultant in Child and Adolescent Psychiatry and
Clinical Director Gwent Health Authority.

Contents

Introduction

IF YOU ARE READING THIS BOOK the chances are that you, or
someone close to you, has been sexually abused or raped.

The sexual abuse of an adult or child is an assault not
only on the body but also on the mind. It engenders a feeling
of alienation, of living in a world which is neither safe
nor accepting.

When rape occurs in adulthood all that was previously
perceived as safe and familiar can become distorted and
threatening. Even the closest relationships can be shattered, with
loved ones becoming objects of fear. The effects of rape can also
reverberate throughout the family, damaging every member.

Childhood sexual abuse (CSA) can determine the way a
child perceives himself and therefore the person he becomes.
The mind takes extraordinarily creative measures to allow him
to function, but being a good partner, parent or social worker
takes more effort from someone struggling with the low self-
esteem, wild mood swings, destructive urges and mistrust
instilled in them while still a child.

People who were sexually abused when they were
children are not, however, a special social group, as is so often
implied by the media. Like so many others who have survived
adversity, they are just people with a traumatic history – they
are as different from each other as the victims of a hurricane.
Indeed, those who transcend severe childhood sexual abuse

will probably never be ordinary. Instead they are extraordinary, with each finding their own unique methods of getting through the bad times. It is a privilege to work with such people, to learn from them and to enjoy the sense of fun and talent for living which so often arise phoenix-like from their suffering.

About This Book

When you first hear a foreign language it is incomprehensible, but as you begin to understand its structure and to master parts of it the rest seems much less daunting. Similarly, the more we understand the nature and effects of our trauma, the less overwhelming it becomes. So within these pages you will find an explanation of rape and child sexual abuse, and of the savage and paralysing feelings which can be the aftermath of sexual assault. You will also find effective, tested methods for reaching deeply into the unconscious mind and changing disabilities into strengths.

Since man could first throw a stone, rape has been a perk of battle. Billions of men and women have been raped and survived to become our ancestors, unwittingly passing on to us their strength and coping mechanisms. They learned to feed their minds with the right messages to allow them both to contain and utilize their pain, their deprivation and their humiliation. In the pages that follow you will find some modern versions of these age-old ways.

Above all, this book seeks to offer a path from understanding to healing, from being buffeted by your emotions to living the life you choose. It is a guide to accompany you on a journey which is essentially your own - a journey which will be as unique as you are.

WHY LINK RAPE AND CHILD SEXUAL ABUSE?
Sexual abuse is sometimes self-perpetuating because the adult who abuses a child teaches her that abuse is what grown-ups do. The majority of victims of CSA abhor abuse and become

vigilant, even over-protective, parents. A minority, however, become abusers and can abuse many children or rape many adults. The evidence indicates that the majority of rapists were abused as children and that those rapists who were abused by women, particularly by their mothers, rape women. Many people who become rape victims when they grow up were sexually abused as children.

PRONOUNS

Pronouns present a problem here. It is very important that no one who has been sexually assaulted feels excluded from these pages. Gay men and straight men rape gay men and straight men. Straight men rape gay and straight women. Gay women rape straight women and gay women. A young boy sexually abused by his mother or a little girl abused by her grandmother can feel that the words do not apply to them if abusers are referred to as 'he' and victims as 'she' or vice versa. However, it would be tedious to repeat 'him or her', 'he or she' throughout the book. Where possible I have avoided pronouns, but where they are used please provide in your mind the appropriate pronoun for you.

TERMS

In this book the term 'sexual abuse' covers *rape, sexual assault* and *sexual abuse of children* and means:

> **Any sexual act performed without the free consent of the participants, and any sexual act involving an adult and a child.**

PART
one

Hurting

1

Rape

WE ARE BEGINNING a revolution in our attitude towards child sexual abuse and rape. Both have been standard forms of behaviour in the past and both still thrive with little comment in some parts of the world today, but many modern societies find them increasingly distasteful and have criminalized sexual behaviour which is no longer considered appropriate. This repudiation of damaging sexual practices gives us the chance to examine and heal their effects.

Despite criminalization, however, aberrant individuals and groups continue to act out the primitive drives which still lurk in our group psyche. Even today, women and children are regarded as legitimate spoils of war: in the Bosnian conflict approximately 40,000 women had been raped by 1998, while 250,000 had been raped in the conflict in Bangladesh. UNICEF estimates that approximately one in six women becomes a rape victim, and a woman is raped every two minutes in the USA. In Australia it is estimated that 30 per cent of women are raped by their husbands. In the UK one in four women has experienced rape or attempted rape, yet of 46,000 women who contacted Rape Crisis organizations in one year, only 3,000 reported their assault to the police.

Overtly in some countries and covertly in others, children are widely used as prostitutes. A Canadian Government Commission estimates that one in six female children is sexually abused before the age of 14. A study in Lima found that 90 per cent of pregnant children had been raped by their fathers or close relatives.

What is Rape?

According to the laws of most countries, rape must involve the use of a penis. Forcing anything other than a penis into the orifice of a non-consenting person is usually classified as 'indecent assault'. Therefore under most legal systems a woman cannot rape another woman, even if an artificial penis is used for penetration. Nor can a woman rape a man, even if she penetrates his rectum with an object representing a penis. It is only within the last few years that some progressive countries have passed laws which acknowledge that men can be raped.

For our purposes I offer the following definition of rape:

Any assault which culminates in an act or acts of unwelcome penetration of the mouth, anus or vagina of either gender by either gender.

The Horror of Rape

Being face to face with a rapist is a terrifying experience. Being face to face with a balaclava even more so, because what we cannot see is more frightening than what we can. The majority of rapes are committed by someone close to the victim, and victims include infants, children, men and old people.

For however long the attack lasts, the rapist has absolute control of the victim. His will is paramount. The effect is like 'breaking' a horse, in which the creature's self-determination is replaced by dependent obedience. Similar methods are used to create obedient children and soldiers. If domination is not followed by dependence, victims can be left in limbo; their sense of having control over their life removed and replaced by a vacuum.

It is often forgotten that a woman who is not aroused does not produce the lubricants necessary to make penetration painless. Vaginal and, with both male and female rape victims, rectal tearing is common.

Some victims are violated in ways other than penetration, including being forced to drink urine, swallow ejaculate or eat faeces. They often feel they are the only ones who have been assaulted in 'that way'.

How Does Rape Harm?

Most of us are fortunate to be raised in the belief that our body is private. We invest it with the qualities of our innermost Self, and when it is violated it feels as though our very being has been occupied and trashed.

Rape shatters the belief that we are safe, plunging us into a world in which we are conscious, all the time, of danger, both real and imagined. Our minds are normally structured to protect us from awareness of non-imminent danger so that we can function. Take away our blinkers and we feel like a mouse in a cat cage. Once we have been caught and injured, we continue to feel like prey. Our brain responds with a rush of chemicals designed to help us escape or defend ourselves, but these become toxic when not used for this purpose. As a result we may feel increasingly unwell, pulsing with frantic energy whenever we feel fear and yet neither running nor fighting.

We may experience relentless replays of the attack in the cinema of our mind, constantly searching the film for details and projecting the image of our rapist(s) onto strangers in the street. It is as if we are held in a time-warp, banished from all that seemed safe before the assault.

The rape of a well-balanced adult will cause post-sexual shock symptoms which may include alienation, agoraphobia, chronic anxiety, panic attacks and illnesses caused by acute stress. When the psychological injury from the rape heals, however, the victim can be as healthy as before the ordeal, with a strong Self which has been developed in combating the experience.

The rape or abuse of a child is different in that many sexually abused children build their experience into their perception of themselves, so that bad feelings are often experienced as their own 'badness'. This happens because of the way we learn about ourselves from the moment we are born.

Children are born unable to distinguish between what is them and what is the outside world. Sucking the thumb creates sensation in the mouth and thumb, whereas sucking a blanket creates sensation only in the mouth. In this way a child learns that she is not her blanket. A child also learns that crying produces food and attention, so she cries when she is hungry or uncomfortable. She experiences herself as the cause of both the food and the comfort, and thus develops the belief that she is the cause of everything that happens around her while remaining unaware of causes from a world beyond her own direct experience.

Because everything children experience involves themselves, they are unable to separate what they feel from what they are. They cannot yet tell the difference between doing and being. Therefore if grown-ups do things to very young children that hurt and feel bad, the children feel as if they caused the events to happen. Something 'bad' happened, therefore they themselves are 'bad'.

Very young children do not yet understand that feelings are not visible. They believe their badness shows and so they feel ashamed. The feeling of shame then shapes their behaviour by reinforcing the original belief that they are not likeable. In turn this can create a defensive, aggressive or cringing attitude towards other people which leads to rejection.

The rape of someone who was abused as a child can activate old self-loathing and guilt as well as release repressed anger from past assaults.

THE MORAL ISSUE

Rape and sexual abuse are not always conveniently clear-cut moral issues. Sometimes there is no despicable 'villain'.

Debby

Shattered by the sudden death of her parents, Debby arranges for Bill, her brother, to come home for the weekend. Bill, who has learning disabilities, is usually a happy, gentle person, but he occasionally has violent episodes. Late at night, Bill, who is disorientated by his parents' death and his unfamiliar surroundings, goes to Debby for a cuddle. The cuddle gets out of control and Debby is raped.

Bill soon reverts to his usual self and tries to comfort Debby's tears. Debby cannot blame Bill, yet now she can neither trust him nor love him. She has no desire to charge him with rape - not that the case would ever get to court - and so, with no valid target for her outrage, Debby blames herself.

Bereaved of her parents and her brother, Debby is left with physical wounds which will heal, but her sense of shock, defilement and loss may stay with her until she obtains professional help or works through a self-healing project.

Bruce

Bruce was 12 when, having been beaten badly and sexually abused by his father, the court awarded custody of him to his mother. She had married another child-abuser, with whom she had a girl, Alice. Alice and Bruce bonded and found protection and love in each other - a love that soon expressed itself in the way they had been taught by their fathers.

By the time Alice was ten she had grown too old to interest her paedophiliac father. Often child abusers are aroused only by children within a specific age group. He left home, leaving Alice feeling bereaved and worthless. Her behaviour brought her to the attention of social workers. When her vaginal scarring was discovered, Bruce was blamed. No one believed Alice's story about her stepfather.

The Consequences of Rape

The consequences of rape differ widely depending on the degree of violence, fear of death, length of ordeal and relation-ship to the rapist. The following information applies where threat, blackmail, drugs or force were used to coerce.

FRIEND RAPE

The most common form of rape is committed, like murder, by someone known and trusted by the victim. Often it follows an evening when the victim is relaxed, possibly by a recreational drug such as alcohol or marijuana.

Sometimes the rapist believes that the victim returns his sexual desire, interpreting friendship and affection as sexual invitation. Refusal is interpreted as sex-play and all facts that do not support the delusion are dismissed. When the victim shatters the false reality, anger may lead to force.

Afterwards, the rapist needs to believe that it was not rape and may behave as if nothing has happened or as if something romantic has taken place which has created an intimate relationship with the victim. If the rapist is a family member, husband, ex-lover, neighbour, close friend or work colleague, the victim may be tempted to buy into one of the delusions. There can be a tendency for the victim to doubt her own perceptions or it might seem easier to accept the rapist's version and re-establish the old relationship. Accepting that the rape did not happen may also appear to offer escape from its traumatic consequences and the use of euphemisms like 'he went a bit over the top' may seem like a way to avoid facing up to the situation. It can be hard to remain detached from an old friend or colleague and it may even feel as if it is the victim who is persecuting the rapist.

If the rape is not reported, however, the rapist may interpret this as permission to do it again or to select another victim as the target of a fantasy love affair. The rapist's self-esteem may be invested in the relationship with the victim and he may so distort this relationship that the truth upsets the balance of a precarious personality, resulting in suicide attempts.

Police involvement may provide the rapist with emotional care via a probation service. This removes the burden of perceived responsibility from the victim, leaving her free to tend to her own needs. There will not necessarily be a prosecution, but the police can be ready to act if there is further harassment.

DATE RAPE

All groups are vulnerable to date rape, although the rape of women by women is either rare or seldom reported.

The date rapist is likely to choose a location such as the back of a car, the home or a deserted outside location which could suggest that the victim had consented to sex. A calculating rapist will avoid marking the victim if at all possible, realizing that it may come to a 'your word against mine' situation. Without physical damage there is no way to prove that intercourse was not by mutual consent.

In large and competitive communities such as universities the fear of disbelief, ridicule and gossip may prevent the victim from reporting the rape.

DRUG RAPE

Some rapists use the drug Rohipnol – commonly known as 'Roofies' – to render their victims incapable of independent action while appearing drunk. Normally prescribed for insomnia, Rohipnol impairs memory, reduces sexual inhibition and has no taste or smell. This makes it ideal for rapists to slip into drinks. Because of this its manufacturers, Hoffman La Roche, are reformulating Rohipnol to turn drinks blue.

The drug is banned in the USA but available globally on the streets. The recipe for this and other dangerous drugs is available on the Internet. While under its influence the victim is aware at some level of what is happening but is powerless to prevent it and afterwards may have only dream-like memories of the rape. Some victims may even doubt their own sanity, as the drug disappears from the body rapidly, leaving no trace for evidence.

Another drug being used is Gamma-Hydroxybutyrate, known as Gamma-OH in Europe. Its properties are similar to Rohipnol and it is also banned in the USA – which of course does not mean that it is not used. In fact it is fairly easy to acquire.

GHB is the drug of choice for those rapists who prefer anal sex, as one of its properties is muscle relaxation.

MEDICAL ABUSE

The medical world – doctors, dentists and therapists – has unique quasi-legitimate access to intimate touching. In such cases, abuse can be disguised so well that the recipient is unsure whether it actually occurred. This can cause the abused person to lose her faith in her own perceptions, which in turn can initiate self-doubt.

People lacking in self-confidence are more likely to be abused in this way than those who are assertive. The very young, the naïve and vulnerable are also targeted, with some practitioners trying to pass off sexual activity as part of the treatment they offer. Often no charges are brought after medical abuse because it cannot be proved, so the abused person learns to shun medical help.

JUVENILE GANG RAPE

Cases of juvenile gang rape are beginning to find their way into the courtrooms of some countries. The perpetrators of particularly vicious gang rapes are usually aged between 10 and 17 years, as are their victims. The physical (one English girl reported being unable to walk properly for several weeks) and mental trauma of the victims is compounded by having to face their rapists at school and on the street.

Unresearched and uncoordinated as this form of rape and child abuse is, it would appear that most of the victims are from low-income groups and their parents do not have the option of removing their children to a different environment where they can recover in relative safety.

OPPORTUNIST RAPE

This seems to be an almost exclusively male crime which is simply committed because the opportunity is there – for instance, when a hitch-hiker is raped. The rapist is unknown to the victim prior to the attack.

Opportunist rapes can occur in isolated or deserted places such as bus shelters, public lavatories, even railway carriages. Vehicle rape can end with the victim abandoned, sometimes far from anything familiar, and left to find her own way back. If the victim is too shocked to take the number of the vehicle, or it has been stolen, prosecution may not be an option, thus leaving the raped person with no target for her anger and faced with the anguish of the ordeal.

PREMEDITATED RAPE

These crimes are often perpetrated by people with obsessive mental disorders or who have a subnormal emotional range. They do not perceive their victims as people but rather as prey carefully selecting and stalking them over a period of time that may range from minutes to years. The rapist's major pleasure is likely to be derived from the victim's suffering and humiliation.

Such a rapist plans and executes the crime with cunning and is often difficult to catch because of the apparently random nature of the rape. In this type of rape disbelief of the victim is not an issue, but fear of death may be a component of the emotional trauma, because murder seems to be a likely outcome at the time.

THE PEER GROUP, SCHOOL MATES, MILITARY COLLEAGUES

Peer group abuse occurs when groups of people conspire to use an individual for sexual amusement, with or without violence, thus violating a trust that humans need in order to function – the belief that we are safe with members of our own 'tribe'.

Being a group victim often seems to confirm the fear that your Self is not acceptable. Someone who is different by virtue of colour, class or gender is more at risk than someone homogeneous with the group. However, even in a seemingly uniform group a difference as small as hair colour may be found and used. Most of us have memories from school-days which illustrate how easy it is to select, or become, a group victim.

Rape or sexual humiliation by groups such as school mates or members of a military regiment can be powerfully shaming and isolating. In institutions such as army training barracks one group member is often selected as the target and subjected to escalating bullying and ridicule. The bullying can culminate in the victim being raped by the group, starting with the most dominant member. For the victim the rape follows a long period of deliberate dismantling of self-esteem.

Group rape often goes unreported because the victim is unable to bear further humiliation. Some victims prefer to leave the group, even when this involves the ignominy of expulsion.

THE RAPE OF POLITICAL DETAINEES OF REPRESSIVE GOVERNMENTS

Political prisoners are often raped as part of the process of 'breaking' them. This kind of rape can be an integral part of systematic torture and interrogation. Maximum pain, humiliation and disorientation are part of the technique, coupled with sleep deprivation and isolation.

Being raped and/or tortured while held in isolation and reviled, with nothing more than memory to sustain a sense of identity and connection to a world where this is not happening, challenges the very foundation of identity. Survivors often transcend the usual tolerance of human beings and gain a compassion and acceptance which may be born of knowing they have survived the worst that life can offer. Sometimes, however, they find a way of being that so far surpasses the norm that their very superiority is isolating.

The West hosts many brave people who have suffered appallingly from the aftermath of torture of which rape was a part. Such refugees may suffer flashbacks, loneliness and disorientation in an unfamiliar community seemingly indifferent to the suffering in their beloved home country.

THE RAPE OF ELDERLY PEOPLE

When elderly people are raped the physical damage is likely to be great because their bodies have lost their resilience. The vaginas of elderly women lose their elasticity. Even when the physical damage is healed, frailty prevents the power-taking aspect of healing open to younger victims because an elderly person's nervous system is less equipped to cope with shock. A sense of safety may never be regained, with the result that precious independence may be lost and the remaining years of the victims' lives spent in isolation and terror.

However, the elderly can reach a position of wisdom which can leave us in awe. I include the statement of a woman of 75. It speaks for itself.

Violet
It was just my body that got hurt and I have long since stopped thinking of my body as 'me'. The perishing thing gets me around, but it is a long time since I have been "Viagra" I don't mind that. Got bored with male display long ago. I thought [my attackers] were going to kill me and I was sorry – I want to see Florida. I said to myself, 'I don't want a willy to be the last thing I see'. They were nice in hospital and kept saying it would

take me time to get over it. Bless them, I haven't got time for getting over things. I'll just have to be like Scarlet O'Hara and cry tomorrow and do the things I want to do today.

So You Were a Prostitute ...

Many young people sell sex. Many as a result of emotional deprivation or extreme poverty. Some have no choice and are kidnapped and sent to other countries where they are forced to have sex with whoever pays for them. This is multiple long-term rape; when children are taken it is also CSA.

Although the media sometimes features forced sex traffic in Latin America and Asia, less is published about young men and women held in Western countries. Often the captives are too brutalized, drug dependent and intimidated to seek help.

There is nothing new about this. The 'white slave trade', as it was known, thrived in nineteenth-century Europe. Young children were dosed with laudanum and shipped out to countries where white skin and virginity were highly prized by powerful and sexually jaded men.

More recently, the social, economic and psychological devastation that has followed the ceasefire in wars such as that in the Balkans is inevitably followed by the provision of young bodies to satisfy the desires of the disturbed populace and the inevitable infestation of criminal profiteers.

Those who survive enforced prostitution can suffer from guilt and self-loathing when their age or physical deterioration finally ends their ordeal. Those who have willingly exchanged sex for money often suffer even more from self-rejection, although they have probably jettisoned their practices because of increased self-respect. Those of us who expose ourselves to risk through sex are likely to have been humiliated and hurt as little children. Are we recreating old emotional conditions by placing ourselves at risk from violent killers and sadists?

Many people have gone on to become fulfilled members of the community after leaving prostitution. Why should they not? A butterfly does not refuse to fly because it was once a caterpillar! What is there to feel guilty about? Probably nothing – compared with violence, theft and cruelty, what we do with our own bodies (unless they are infectious) must surely be a mere misdemeanour, if that. Society's undoubted prejudice should be challenged, because, undeniably, there is a stigma to prostitution.

In countries which are poor or where the wealth is jammed into the bank accounts of the few, prostitution may be the difference between life and death for many families. In Guatemala I have seen young mothers take their four-year-old children to perform fellatio on tourists. Without the income from their child's exploitation, the whole family could starve. Who should feel shame, the child, the tourist or the politicians?

Kuko

Kuko was raised in Manchuria. The Japanese invaded when she was 11. She saw most of her family die but she was spared to be used as a 'comfort woman' for the Japanese troops. She became the special 'property' of a high-ranking officer who took her with him when he returned to Tokyo.

When the war ended Kuko was left alone in Tokyo, where, to survive, she sold all she had, her little body. She had a regular client who was in the US army. He found her intelligent and musically talented and became so fond of her that they married.

When Kuko returned to the States with her new husband she was warmed by the welcome she received from her mother-in-law and came to trust her. This led to her telling her life story. The older woman reacted with righteous shock horror and Kuko was told to leave the house. This time she was not penniless, but she had no emotional support from her husband, who may have chosen her for her childlike quality (which she was losing), and she was pregnant.

When her son was born Kuko's husband told her that she would not be allowed to keep him because the law said that prostitutes are unfit mothers. He and his mother took charge of the child and Kuko was alone again. Eventually she became a singer, never famous but rarely out of work. Now well into her sixties, she works with a rape centre and gives her love to her cats, who do not judge her.

Reporting Rape

When it is difficult to prove rape it sometimes feels as if it is not worth the hassle of reporting it to the police. However, it is not uncommon to regret making the decision not to report rape, especially if the rapist gloats, sneers and generally seems to feed emotionally on the crime. The decision about reporting should also take into account the degree of sophistication of your particular police force.

Some people choose to take legal action out of a sense of duty to other potential victims. Others do so to channel their anger into the prosecution of the abuser and regain their own sense of power. Sometimes this has proved to be all the therapy they need: caring professionals have helped them tell their story and shared their sense of outrage, and society has validated their feelings by appropriate sentencing. However, there are those who have been intimidated by the notorious judicial mishandling of some rape cases in which judges have re-abused the victim in their summing up.

Recently pressure groups and the media have done much to change archaic legal attitudes to sexual crime and it is now widely acknowledged that no one should have to defend their right to wear what they like, where and when they like, or to have had a sex life before they were raped. In some countries it is no longer possible for the victim to be cross-examined by the rapist and children are allowed to give evidence on video so that they do not have to confront their abuser.

A good police force rarely prosecutes in cases where there is serious doubt about the outcome. A decision not to prosecute does not imply disbelief, but that the evidence is inadequate. It is not always worth risking a 'not guilty' verdict, with all that that would imply for the complainant.

2

Child Sexual Abuse

What is Child Sexual Abuse?

In this book child sexual abuse is defined as:

> **An act involving genital contact between an adult and a child, or between a child and a more powerful child, unless that contact is for appropriate medical or hygienic purposes.**

To understand the origins of child sexual abuse we need to look at the way our species has evolved. Survival is the priority of every species and human survival once meant procreation at the earliest possible moment. Girls were (and still are in some cultures) fertilized before they menstruated. Ancient writings tell us that early Middle Eastern tribes permitted sex with girls of three years and one day. The Ancient Greeks regarded sex with young boys as a normal part of a man's life and some boys were castrated to keep them looking youthful. Even in the USA marriages of 13-year-old children took place in the latter half of the twentieth century. It is possible that in the last 2,000 years more children under 16 have been used sexually than have not.

Why Does Sex Damage a Child?

Children are naturally tactile and, if not imbued with shame, enjoy experimenting with the sensations they can produce in their own bodies. This is a type of play and is practice for growing up, just as kittens learn to hunt by playing with a toy. However, because a child is ready to experiment with bodily sensations, this does not mean he is ready for sex with an adult. A four-year-old child may play with a doll, but this does not mean she is ready for childbirth. A child may play with a toy gun, but he is not ready to go to war. Sex, killing and childbirth are major emotional experiences which are too powerful for a developing mind to process.

The inequality of the adult/child relationship and the premature release of sexual needs can freeze a child's emotional development. When an aroused abuser hurts a child physically, the child can believe the sex is a punishment for being 'bad'. This is understandable, as the physical manifestation of anger – flushed face, muscle tension, excited demeanour – is very similar to sexual arousal. The child may then act from the shame of her 'badness' until the early experiences are revisited and seen through adult eyes.

For a child coerced into sex by force or threats, sex and terror may become inseparable. This can create adults trapped in an addiction to violent relationships or, alternatively, sexually paralysed by terror and therefore leading sexless lives.

How Can Parents Sexually Abuse their Children?

An abused child may grow into an adult whose intellectual and physical development is exceptional, while emotionally it remains as vulnerable and uncontrolled as a young child. This can be charming in some people but dangerous in others. When a person whose emotional development has 'frozen' in this way becomes a parent he may be emotionally younger than his own children.

Humans have a powerful unconscious drive to reconstruct the circumstances of childhood, even when consciously striving to do the opposite. Unconsciously we search for aspects of our parents when selecting our partners. Some of us search for the pleasant qualities and some, without being aware of it, for the unpleasant. A sexually abusive parent is an immature creature, obsessed with self-gratification, for whom others are but bit players in the drama of his life. The child of such a parent is in danger of selecting a partner who is also trapped in that self-orientated period of childhood. Children of abusers who have unwittingly chosen an abuser as a partner report a feeling of familiarity and bonding from the first meeting.

When two people who have both been abused have children, there is a risk that if both are trapped in their own drama and controlled by their toxic memories, they will re-enact their childhoods. One parent may perfect the art of believing conflicting truths. One or both may be fixated on sex with children. Both have grown up with child abuse as their norm and, as parents, may collude consciously or unconsciously to continue the cycle of abuse. 'It never hurt me' is a common justification made by those with too much invested in a positive self-image to allow for doubt. One partner is likely to be dependently fixated on the other in the same way that a young child is emotionally dependent upon a parent (*see* Stockholm Syndrome, page 76). For them, keeping their abusive partner becomes a self-flagellatory obsession, a 'god' to which all else, including their children, can be sacrificed.

Such couples represent a tiny proportion of those abused as children, but they are sufficient to maintain the cycle of child abuse.

Irene

Irene had four children including identical twin boys. The sexual behaviour of Bill, her latest partner, with her children became increasingly inappropriate. When Irene, consumed with jealousy, complained, Bill threatened to leave. Terrified of losing him,

Irene 'gave' him one of the twins to abuse. When the child's injuries were noticed at school Bill was arrested. Irene attacked her son violently, both verbally and physically, blaming him for her lover's imprisonment, her unhappiness and the family's shame.

Not all abusers' partners are collusive and not all collusive partners are consciously so. One abuser can abuse hundreds of children. It is important to recognise that most abused children do not grow up to abuse, rather that nearly all abusers have been abused.

Incest

The incest taboo probably evolved to avoid breeding from a restricted gene pool. When we breed from a small gene pool we increase the chances of replicating genetic disadvantages, such as inherited diseases, as well as the chances of replicating advantages such as good eyesight. Some other mammals have also developed ways to prevent breeding with close relatives, except in circumstances where the alternative is not to breed at all.

Early societies consisted of fewer people and the results of inbreeding were more obvious. We know from the strict laws laid down in the Bible (Leviticus 18) that the early Semites had observed the consequences of inbreeding. The Semites' neighbours and one-time conquerors, the Egyptians, practised incest, having some understanding that breeding from close relatives retains family traits. With serial pregnancies and limited medical facilities, physically and mentally disadvantaged babies tended to die, as they do in some countries today, leaving those with genetic advantages for future breeding.

Ancient legends, such as that of Zeus raping his mother, seem uncritical of incest. Then opinion seems to have changed and cautionary dramas emerged, such as that of Oedipus, who blinded himself following his marriage to his mother. We can see similar changes in values happening today. A couple of decades ago drunken driving was considered by many to be a bit of laugh. Now it is unacceptable to the majority.

WHY DOES INCEST CARRY SUCH SHAME?
Because incest has become taboo in the West, the word alone is enough to generate feelings of shame and worthlessness. The vilification associated with incest has become more harmful to the victim than the transgressor. The victim can be left with excruciating shame for something which was not her responsibility and which has harmed no one else.

If we strip away the shame, we can see that incest may carry some genetic risks to offspring and that parent/child incest robs the child of the chance to develop naturally. Children of incestuous liaisons who are adopted are often healthy and well-adjusted as long as they do not know their parentage; many remain that way even when they do know.

If you are a child or victim of incest, remember you have harmed no one and have no grounds for guilt. Your task is to learn all you can about the subject. Knowledge will lessen any irrational self-loathing.

Jasmine
Jasmine's mother was an invalid and her father had told her that it was her duty to do the things her mother was unable to do, including have sex with him. He used force as well as emotional blackmail. Jasmine's shame caused unusual behaviour which isolated her and prevented her from forming friendships. As a result, she was effectively alone in the world when her mother threw her out of the house on discovering the sexual relationship. That was when Jasmine discovered that she had been adopted. The freedom she felt from the guilt of her supposed incest freed her to work on the other aspects of her abuse.

Teresa

Teresa's father was in the British army. He married a very young girl from a simple Middle Eastern farming community. Back in his cottage in a remote part of Wales he became bored by his wife, whose dress marked her apart, as did her inability to master English, and the marriage soon failed. When Teresa was born her father left.

Mother and baby were isolated. The mother would quieten Teresa by rubbing her genitals and the two shared a bed and many intimacies. Having met very few people Teresa was terrified by school and her mother often found reasons to keep her at home. This eventually brought a visit from the authorities which frightened the mother so much that she banned Teresa from her bed.

Teresa reacted badly, screaming to be allowed back until she eventually was. She remained isolated at school, enduring the day, waiting only to return to the presence of her mother. Teresa never made friends and the intimacies between mother and daughter continued into Teresa's teens. She then experienced a healthy revulsion for her mother and demanded her own bed and a TV in the flat.

One day, during an argument, Teresa stabbed her mother with a pair of nail scissors. She did not hurt her badly, but was so distressed that she ran away. When she returned a few days later she found that her mother had killed herself.

Teresa was so disturbed that she was sectioned and while in hospital the history of her relationship with her mother was uncovered. Eventually she joined a therapeutic community where she found she could heal at her own pace and in safety.

How Does Child Sexual Abuse Harm?

There are similarities in the way sexually abused children develop, but there are also differences arising from the age of the child at the time of abuse, the gender of the abuser, whether the abuse was painful or pleasurable, and the relationship of the abuser to the child.

MOTHER/DAUGHTER

This form of abuse usually occurs in early childhood, making a normal mother/child relationship impossible, and so the child is deprived of emotional nourishment and security.

The ensuing love-hate bond between mother and daughter is not easily broken. Even as an adult the victim can feel possessed by her mother, as if there is no demarcation between their identities. Respectful boundaries between parent and child, and an acknowledgement of the child's separateness, are essential for the child to become a self-determining individual. The invasion of the child's Self can result in a loathing of her mother's body being experienced as loathing of her own. This loathing can extend to all female bodies.

FATHER/DAUGHTER

The fundamental need for a protective father can never be fulfilled by a sexually abusive father. A new father figure – one who respects personal boundaries – is needed. If the child is very young and the sex is confused with love, there is a danger that the daughter will seek the characteristics of the abusive 'father' in prospective partners. This can be the blueprint for a life of decreasing self-esteem packed with broken and abusive relationships.

FATHER/SON

The dominance and abuse of power here can leave the boy feeling robbed of his self-determination and masculinity. He has no father in his life, just a big, abusive child wearing a man's body. As a result, all masculine influence may become polluted. Fear and shame can cause the boy to shun input from the outside world and to develop within himself instead. Often such people are referred to as 'living in a world of their own', because communication is difficult both for them and with them.

Sometimes the impact of the sexual activity can be so powerful that the boy identifies his own sexual orientation as homosexual when in reality it is heterosexual. This can condemn him to a series of sexual encounters in which he may unconsciously re-enact the sex with his father. These encounters can leave him feeling empty and used. The boy who is truly gay may well find joy and fulfilment in a same-sex relationship; the heterosexual cannot.

In adulthood the victim of this kind of abusive relationship may become violent and aggressive while feeling that he is barely defending himself. He may be driven to 'prove his masculinity' by having many heterosexual encounters but few relationships. His need to be accepted as a man may lead to a life spent in pubs or to joining organizations which stress macho characteristics, such as the army, or street gangs.

MOTHER/SON

If a little boy's sexual curiosity is satisfied by sexual contact with his mother, his drive to form outside relationships does not fully develop. The boy often becomes sexually dependent on his mother and finds other sexual relationships unsatisfying.

In adulthood, such men can be obsessed with their mothers into old age. In some cases, even if the man marries and has children, his primary relationship remains with his mother. A tragic result of this abuse can be that the man never leaves his mother's home and nurses her into her very old age, only to be devastated by her death.

USE BY BOTH PARENTS AS A SEX TOY

When a child is betrayed by both parents it is effectively orphaned. Its inclusion in its parents' intimate lives also creates a false equality which the child is too young to handle. Obviously the child has no choice in its sexual development and its ability to develop naturally is destroyed.

Eventually the child may learn that its life is abnormal and repugnant to the outside world. The process of experiencing Self as separate from parents is difficult enough in standard lives, but for the sex-toy child it may never happen. The natural process of reaching out to friends and developing new aspects of Self is impaired. At worst the child may be condemned to life as little more than a psychological foetus, bound to its parents for all its needs unless life presents an opportunity for healing.

The extreme pathology of parents who treat their children in this way renders them incapable of parenting in other ways. The experience of parents as protective mentors is therefore denied to the child until such time as the relationship can be synthesized or replaced.

BROTHER/SISTER, BROTHER/BROTHER, SISTER/SISTER

Incest between siblings is often damaging when it is not by mutual choice or when the instigator is much more powerful. The damage from voluntary sexual relations between siblings is often caused by guilt at having broken the incest taboo. It is felt to be something darkly shameful in a way that sex with non-family members would not be. However, a certain amount of sexual curiosity and voluntary speculation between siblings is common and does not necessarily impact on the children's emotional development.

GRANDPARENTS AND OTHER FAMILY MEMBERS

Because a significant part of abusive behaviour is based on power and addiction there is no such thing as being 'too old' to be an abuser. Being too old to penetrate does not prevent other sexual behaviour.

Grandparents who abuse their grandchildren are likely to have been paedophilic all their adult lives and may well have abused the child's parent. It is very important that the next generation is protected, and so this type of abuse needs airing within the family because many members may be holding secrets, all feeling they are the 'only one'.

PASTORAL FIGURES

Pastoral abuse of a child shatters his confidence in the outside world and also impedes childhood exploration and growth within the community. Often the reason that the abuse continues is that the child does not have sufficient confidence in his parents to tell them. If the abuser is a person revered or feared by the parents – a teacher, priest or other authority figure – then the child experiences the parents, and by inference himself, as powerless. To the child, the abuser outranks the parents.

Such abusers often use their power in the community to refute allegations. Who would take the word of a disturbed child against that of a high-ranking police officer? Who would take the word of a disturbed adult against that of a priest counsellor?

Some paedophiles are obsessed with their sexual yearnings to the extent that they design their lives to fulfil them, choosing their job to facilitate their perversion. Foster-parenting and home-making to children in care offer the opportunities they crave. Hurt by the breakdown in her family life prior to being placed in care, the child suffers from loss, which may be compounded by a sense of rejection. She is desperate for attention, not to be just one of a crowd. The need to be hugged, to be listened to, to be special is easily exploited.

When the paedophile is also sadistic the child lives in fear as well as misery. Some child abusers use religion to justify their abuse and to instil a deep guilt in the children in their care.

Many authorities are improving the supervision of residential care in the wake of the many recent exposures of this type of abuse. This augurs well for the future, but leaves many deprived and miserable adults trying to manage life in the outside world. If, during childhood, their most basic emotional needs were met before they were institutionalized, they will have suffered bereavement for what they have lost. If their basic emotional needs were never met, they were deprived of the chance of maturing emotionally, yet in their teens were turned out into a world which demanded they behave as adults, without the support of family or adequate inner resources.

YOUNG ABUSERS

Paedophiles are frequently fixated on children in a particular age-group, which can lead to an abused child becoming 'too old' and being dropped for a younger child. This 'rejection' can produce explosive anger and sexual frustration in the child who, seeing herself as inadequate, needs to find a source of feeling powerful. This may be achieved by the abuse of other children. This behaviour gains the child an odium which reinforces the sense of being unlovable.

Sexual curiosity can also lead children, particularly those who are in puberty, to experiment with children in their care. Children may put up with the abuse from older children because they feel included and grown up. They may also be intimidated by threats, believing that they, not the older children, will be blamed if the abuse is uncovered.

GROOMED ABUSE

Some abusers befriend their victims to engender their dependence and/or trust with the purpose of violating them. Wealthy men befriend young boys; couples open their home to troubled girls; self-appointed gurus offer dubious 'help' to disturbed youngsters. Lonely young people are selected and 'groomed' for abuse because they are too alienated from society to feel entitled to its protection.

Pregnant Children

Children who become pregnant from abuse can be surprisingly resilient, often postponing their reaction until adulthood, although the pregnancy itself is likely to separate them further from their peers, effectively ending their childhood.

In some countries pregnant children are driven from their homes to fend for themselves. If they live in a society which does not permit abortion and they are forced to give birth to a baby which is then adopted, they may well spend the rest of their lives wondering what became of their child. Children have been known to give birth without their parents even knowing they were pregnant. Some of these children have killed their babies as soon as they are born. Some parents may elect for abortion without telling their daughter that she is pregnant, while others choose to raise the child as their own.

What Happens When Sexual Abuse of a Child Within the Home is Reported?

The procedures in these cases differ from country to country and depend on funding and the skills of social workers. In the West when sexual abuse within the family is reported, social workers have a duty to ensure that the child is safe. What happens next depends on whether or not the offending parent leaves the home.

If the offending parent does leave, the child is sometimes allowed to return. If the non-offending parent believes the child, and acts protectively towards him, returning home is usually the best option. Some good parents suppress their own distress and make their abused child their priority, but even so the child risks returning to a home full of misery, shock and anxiety for which he may feel responsible. Some parents may resent the child for breaking up the family, alternately believing and disbelieving his account of what has happened. Brothers and sisters may also blame the child, or feel jealous of the one chosen to be 'special' by the abusive parent.

If the abuser is found guilty, a prison sentence usually follows, but the child knows that the abuser may not be away for very long and may return to the family home after release. The abused child may also feel responsible for the imprisonment.

If the abuser does not leave the family home the child is often placed elsewhere – in residential care or a foster home – while enquiries are made. If there is sufficient evidence to prosecute the abuser, the child is likely to remain in care until the case has come to court, which can take months. In some cases the child may not receive therapy before a court hearing for fear that the therapist might influence the way he remembers events.

Some residential homes are well funded and staffed by caring experts, but others are less well run. There is also the risk of unsophisticated children being housed with street-wise youngsters whose behaviour mimics their violent past and whose attitude to unworldly newcomers is likely to be less than kind.

The alternative to residential care is fostering, although in some places the number of children needing foster homes far exceeds the good homes available. While some children have been re-abused in foster homes, others have been placed with trained foster parents and found the stable, loving environment they need for recovery.

In the worst case scenario the child is rejected by the non-abusing parent, sent to a residential centre, bullied by tougher residents, then placed in a series of unsatisfactory foster homes. Her behaviour becomes unacceptable and she returns to residential care until reaching the age at which society expects her to care for herself, usually 16.

Many abused children who have fled their homes can be found begging on the streets of the world's cities. Shelter, an organization for the homeless in the UK, tells us that homeless youngsters are frequently re-abused by adults offering food or warmth in return for sexual favours.

The Wounds of Childhood Sexual Abuse

We are complex creatures, difficult to predict or categorize, and we each react to injury in different ways. Listed below are some of the contradictory ways in which we may respond to being sexually abused as children. First, however, it is important to point out that having these symptoms is not of itself confirmation of sexual abuse. They can all arise from other experiences.

Self-perception

- *seeing your body as much fatter or thinner than it is*
- *perceiving yourself as sexually irresistible*
- *perceiving yourself as ugly and unattractive*
- *not being sure of your sexual orientation*
- *feeling hollow, as if there is no 'real you'*
- *loathing yourself*
- *feeling powerless*
- *believing others to have an 'X' factor missing from your Self*

Physical signs

- *a posture which hides the breasts and/or genitals*
- *hair hiding the face*
- *being overweight*
- *being underweight*
- *wearing sexy clothes without experiencing them as such*
- *wearing body-hiding clothes*
- *unconsciously adopting a posture that proffers the genitals*
- *wearing heavy make-up*
- *presenting yourself as childlike*

Sexual symptoms

- *disgust at all sexual activity*
- *frequent, short-lived relationships*
- *experiencing the presence of the abuser during sex*

- *a compulsion to comply with sexual demands from people to whom you are not attracted*
- *the need to fantasize the Self or the partner as a child during sex*
- *a fear of abusing children*
- *no sexual feelings*
- *unconsciously selecting a partner who 'forces' extreme sexual behaviour*
- *pain during sexual intercourse with no medical cause*
- *being unaware of your own sexually inviting behaviour and being devastated by the response to it*
- *priapism (persistent erections)*
- *attraction to elderly people*
- *cutting the penis – your own and others*
- *casual sex with strangers*
- *impotence*

Other symptoms

- *choosing partners to abuse your Self with*
- *choosing exploitative friends*
- *seeking to become a member of another family*
- *being a victim of rape or violence*
- *spending a large proportion of time in fantasy*
- *having friends who have been sexually abused*
- *feeling powerless to stop yourself being unpleasant to your partner*
- *having a homosexual relationship when your desire is heterosexual*
- *having heterosexual encounters when your desire is homosexual*
- *having a nurturing job such as a nurse or social worker*
- *substance dependence*
- *frequent nightmares*

- *cutting and burning the body, or hurting it in other ways, to obtain relief from misery*
- *amnesia of long periods of childhood*
- *self-sabotage (unconscious) of career, relationships, health*
- *frequent spontaneous trance (daydreaming)*
- *difficulties with boundaries in relationships*
- *living in conflicting realities – for example, 'I have a happy marriage' versus 'I'm miserably married'*
- *flashbacks*

Some of these symptoms are, or can be made into, positive traits. Others perpetuate feelings and/or activities which can be both savage and agonizing; the sense of fear and shame these create is no less difficult to bear because it is unfounded.

PART
two

Healing

3

Preparing to Heal

IF YOU HAVE BEEN traumatized by sexual assault you may feel trapped by what happened, be experiencing flashbacks and feeling that you have lost, or have never had, control of your life. Yet history teaches us that generations of those harmed by sexual exploitation have found ways to overcome their traumatic experience. In doing so they have provided us with rich healing resources upon which to draw for our own healing.

Healing takes time and hard work, but it can be exciting, sometimes breathtakingly so. How long and how difficult your task will be depends upon how deeply you have been harmed. You can liken it to being underwater. If you are snorkling on the surface, coming up is fast and easy. If you are scuba diving, it will take longer and need more skill. If you are deep-sea diving, you need more time and you cannot do it alone. It is your responsibility to yourself and others to be realistic about the depth of your injury. It is easy to overestimate the depth in order to give yourself an alibi for staying the way you are. It is also easy to underestimate your fragility out of misplaced shame.

Your objective is not to become perfect. If you have been raped, your objective is to be as you were before the rape, but stronger and wiser. If you were abused as a child, your objective is to rid yourself of the feelings and behaviour caused by the abuse and claim the talents and well-being that are yours by right.

Many people who have become champions took up their particular sport in order to overcome a physical disadvantage, and many actors began their studies to overcome a speech impediment. You, too, can turn your disadvantage into advantage by gaining access to your inner world and turning it into a comfortable and attractive place to live.

The fact that you are reading this book means that you are already seeking to heal. Your next step is to adapt the coping strategies you developed in childhood. They served you well, they got you this far.

Children, like our early ancestors, seem to know how to survive major hurts. Watch a scolded child correct his teddy, thus reliving his bad experience from a position of power. Watch a frightened child comfort her doll. Do you remember making insulting drawings of teachers you disliked? Instinctively children use methods which 'experts' have rediscovered and consider state of the art.

Some of your old healing ways may not be appropriate in their present form, but they are flexible and can change with you. If you were an abused child you can start changing the way you think by owning that you are about as helpless as a Sherman tank. If you were not made from tough genetic material you would not be here to read this now, so great can be the impact of sexual abuse upon a child.

Scar tissue is stronger than undamaged tissue. You can think of emotional 'scar tissue' in the same way. When you have healed you will be especially strong emotionally. How often have you heard of people who changed dramatically for the better after severe personal trauma? You have had the trauma, now it is time for change. Remember, you will never be ordinary, but you can become extraordinary.

One of the main defence mechanisms developed by

sexually abused children is the ability to escape into fantasy. It is also one of the strategies used by victims of rape, because shock can produce a dream-like feeling that assists imagination. By harnessing together the qualities of imagination and absolute honesty you can transcend your suffering and use it as fertilizer for your future growth. You can feed your unconscious with the positive, strengthening experiences that may have been missing from your childhood. You can also express your anger, fear or despondency about your abuse, instead of reacting inappropriately to events in the present. Think of it as taking out the splinter rather than treating the swelling.

You can also admit that it is unlikely that Fate has singled you out for punishment and that you cannot change the world, but you will change yourself. It is unfair that you should have to do this work. But then life is not fair. Whoever said it was?

First Steps

Start by imagining your mind to be a troubled country which is suffering the aftermath of invasion and famine. There are casualties who need assistance, starving people to be fed and much of the infrastructure needs to be repaired or even redesigned. Think of yourself as embarking upon a mission. You know that peace and plenty cannot be achieved at once but that if you work on the priorities the rest will become easier. Expect setbacks – this is a land where things do not always go according to plan. However, you know you must persevere. Giving up is not an option.

The more you know about sexual abuse, the better equipped you will be for your task. Information about rapists and abusers, about incest and prostitution, if these are relevant, will help you to put your life in context and to challenge any irrational feelings of guilt or isolation. Other essential equipment is persistence, courage and commitment.

WAYS AND MEANS

The techniques offered in the following pages are designed to help you to change the way you feel and act. A good cow knows exactly which plants to select from the meadow when it is sick. You too have the ability to choose the right cure for yourself. Try all the techniques and use the ones that feel right, that intrigue you. If some feel wrong, don't use them.

That we have the ability to heal is in no doubt, but healing major trauma requires a serious commitment. It is not something to do in odd moments when there is nothing on TV. Healing involves retraining your mind and practising new ways of being until they feel automatic. If you are training a dog to walk to heel, you cannot let it pull sometimes. Each time you do, you are teaching it to pull.

You will find frequent use of imagery in the following techniques. Imagery is powerful because it is the way we store our memories. It is also the way children think when they are too little to use language. Imagery developed before language. It is the language of the unconscious mind. As such, it has the power to release emotion.

Some of the exercises involve drawing or modelling. The purpose here is not to produce a 'good' drawing, so do not use not being able to draw as an excuse not to heal! Drawing when you are not skilled helps you to access deep feelings from a time when you had even fewer drawing skills, when you were a child. If you have a talent for drawing, you might like to do the exercises with your non-dominant hand. Drawing also necessitates filling out details in your imagination. For example, just to draw shoes will not do. You have to decide whether they are boots or sandals. What colour are they?

Even more powerful than imagination alone is to draw your improved way of handling the situation as a comic strip, because this can involve using more of your senses.

For the writing exercises, an alternative could be making a tape recording.

The more detailed your 'mind films' are, the deeper the

healing. The more of your senses you use in your work – sight, sound, smell, touch, taste and emotion – the better the result.

TOOLS

One of the first things you will need is a healing journal. This should be an A3-sized book with blank pages. A scrapbook is ideal, but it must be beautiful because it must give you pleasure when you see it. That way you will associate healing with pleasure. It should be a token of the respect that you expect from your Self and others from now on. Buy a beautiful book or buy a plain book and make a cover for it. You will also need a set of felt-tip pens, unless you prefer to paint. The use of colour is important.

Assessing Your Task

Your first project is self-assessment. It may be that you will find working through this book is enough to help you make the changes you want. However, you might decide that you also need the support of professionals or voluntary groups.

Don't be tempted to cheat in the self-assessment. If you do you could be setting yourself up to fail and that is falling into one of the sexual abuse traps. Answer the following questions with clinical honesty. No one but you need know your answers.

1   *How hurt are you? Are you too wounded right now to handle a course of healing alone?*

2   *Are you so wounded that you and your mind are no longer in partnership?*

3   *Are you suicidal?*

4   *Are you experiencing hallucinations?*

5   *Are people you meet aware that you have difficulties?*

6   *Do you foresee your future being as bleak as the present?*

If the answer to the last five questions is 'yes' or even 'maybe', please enlist the support of your physician before you go any further. Not to do so is to risk hurting yourself even more. You can also begin building a therapeutic team – for instance, a therapist can support you while you work through the book, your doctor can protect you with some medication and a voluntary organization can be there for you when you need to talk. Read Chapter 11, choose your team carefully and continue.

Assessing Your Advantages

If you were abused as a child you may be tempted to answer the following questions negatively. This exercise can be a healing step if you do it objectively and resist the temptation to disparage your Self. The object is to take a realistic look at the resources you bring to your project.

1   *List five qualities you would seek in a friend.*

1a *Which of these qualities do you possess?*

2   *What crimes or acts do you most loathe (cruelty to children, drunken driving, arms dealing, hunting, drug dealing)?*

2a *Do you do any of these things?*

3   *What behaviour or habits have you changed (smoking, nail biting)?*

3a *What personal strengths helped you to achieve that?*

4   *How do you show your kindness?*

5   *What is the bravest thing you have ever done? (Something seemingly ordinary to others but difficult for you is fine.)*

6   *Which of your characteristics would you most like to pass on to a child?*

7   *What positive qualities do you bring to your task?*

Change

Think of ten things which change beyond recognition, like caterpillar to butterfly, clouds to rain, bare twig to blossom. All your images must be positive. Fill two of the pages in your book with them. These images can be drawn, cut from magazines, or, better still, how would you like to do them? Focusing on creative change will prime your unconscious mind to make its own changes.

The House of Self

Think of your Self as a house, constructed storey by storey. If the foundations are not strong the house can never be secure.

Ideally, the foundations should be built from security, love, safe touching and attention in a harmonious environment. If the foundations are made from faulty materials, the ground floor will tilt. Similarly, an emotionally malnourished baby will become a troubled toddler, over-compliant or racked by savage emotion.

The next floor will sit precariously upon the ground floor beneath. It may well be superbly decorated and furnished, but it is still only as secure as its foundations. The child may adapt his behaviour to control the toddler's impulses, but fear and fury lie just below the surface.

When the roof is in position the entire structure of the house of Self balances on its foundations, now mostly buried from view. The roof of the house may be spectacular, arousing the admiration of observers, but it can be endangered by the foundations. Though someone may be extremely successful they may be driven by a sense of inadequacy which may one day overwhelm them while their successes crash around them.

If the roof of an otherwise sound house is damaged, the house will stand firm while repairs are made. Sexual attacks on a previously balanced adult can be repaired more easily than those on a child. This in no way diminishes the pain of adults who are assaulted. What it does do is augur well for a recovery which will leave the adult stronger than before the attack.

If your house of Self has been besieged on all levels, you will have carried out repairs and modifications to keep your structure standing, possibly creating an unusual and fascinating edifice in the process. You may well value your quirky and creative house of Self and decide to keep the design while you repair your foundations, yet repair them you must.

If this is to be a DIY job you will work very hard indeed, but remember that even the most stubborn DIY enthusiast is prepared to call in professionals when the work is specialized. It is no failure to seek professional help.

Removing Old Blocks to Recovery

DON'T WANT TO TALK ABOUT IT ...

Some people may feel unable to work therapeutically with another person because their shame and embarrassment are so agonizingly strong that they dread having to use the words for what was done to them. This applies to children as well as adults. Many people believe that making children repeat what has been done to them is a form of abuse. Maybe we are all children when it comes to talking about what embarrasses us the most.

A good therapist will not insist on a detailed account of your abuse. Instead he will work with what you are comfortable with and focus on your emotions rather than on events. For instance, when you say, 'He did those things,' you have a memory 'on screen' and the words 'those things' are as powerful for you as descriptive detail, so the therapist might ask, 'What were you feeling when he did those things?' If talking about your abuse brings release, a therapist may help you to talk about the details, but few therapists will demand to know them. It is destructive to make yourself talk about the abuse while doing so feels very difficult.

THE FEAR OF BEING UNFAIR TO PARENTS

Children bond to their parents with superglue and have been known to run away from loving foster parents to return to vicious natural parents. So, when adults attempt to get in touch with childhood pain they can feel disloyal, even though they know consciously that anger is not the same as blame and that expressing it cannot hurt a parent who will never know. Perhaps there is deep fear of losing the precious illusion of having a good parent. Perhaps it seems to confirm the victims' fear of being unlovable. Sometimes adults establish a good relationship with parents who were unable to relate to them as children. If the new relationship is precious or the parents are frail, anger can feel very dangerous. That is why all anger work must be directed towards the parents *as they were at the time of the abuse, not as they are now.*

CLINGING TO BEING A VICTIM

Some people cling to the belief that they are unable do things other people can do. Just why they cannot do them is never clear, other than 'it is too difficult'. They see fear as an impenetrable block rather than a belief to be dismantled. They set up therapists to fail, explaining that it is too painful to work. They become ill and have to be cared for, or become suicidal and must be rescued. The prison they thus create for themselves is a familiar one, in many ways comfortable and very scary to leave. Just like hens released from battery cages, they will try to return to the only cage they know. The world outside, with its dangers and challenges, is unknown and therefore seems very threatening. Unconsciously they believe they have no identity other than that of the victim and will receive no attention other than that which being a victim brings.

Sam

Sam met his wife, Iris, in group therapy. Sexually and physically abused as a child, Sam had never felt loved and so had few good experiences as resources to draw upon. By the time he was 17 he was dependent on alcohol and amphetamines to block off his self-loathing. A motorcycle accident left him minus a leg and with other injuries which kept him hospitalized for many months and for the first time in his life he found himself the centre of attention. Nurses, physicians, occupational and physiotherapists, and the counsellors who worked with him seemed to care about him and be interested in him.

When it was time for Sam to leave hospital he was found accommodation, given a social worker and eventually found a place in a training college, which he promptly lost. He found it too difficult to get himself there in the morning. It was after several such episodes that he joined the therapeutic group where he met Iris, who was partially sighted. After they married Iris was promoted and earned a good salary while Sam lost job after job. He believed himself to be too nervous to mix with others and he left the group because he experienced it as hostile. Gradually he stopped trying to find work and Iris paid the bills.

Because he was lonely at home while Iris worked long hours Sam spent more and more time in the pub. Iris took on extra work until one day, physically and nervously exhausted, she told Sam, 'Move out, get a job, come back when you are solvent.' Sam took a couple of overdoses and contacted the Samaritans, who listened as he told his story. He felt real sympathy from them as he told of his childhood and accident. When he told of the cruel way Iris had treated him, he heard for the first time the self-deception and self-pity in his words.

Sam found help and began to confront his fear instead of accepting it as insurmountable. He drew it as a thick wall and imagined what might be beyond it. Every time he achieved something difficult he rubbed out one of the concrete blocks that formed the wall and filled in part of the new view. He was lonely and it was difficult, but after a while he began to make new acquaintances, some of whom gradually became friends. He noticed they did not nurture him and he observed something *new in their attitude — respect! He and Iris have now begun to see each other once a week. Whether they live together again remains to be seen, but Sam no longer lives on an emotional diet of pity.*

Practical Work

Earlier we saw that stories can prime the mind for change. Read the therapeutic story 'Space', which follows, experiencing it as if you were the little planet. In your book draw the parts of the story that had the greatest impact on you. Tape record the story and play it to yourself as you relax and visualize the action. Try playing some 'spacey' music in the background as you record.

SPACE

The moment you close your eyes you are in your inner space. The instant your lashes touch you are aware of the limitless space of your mind. To journey into your own mind is to be free, no longer restricted by time or possibility. Know that within the depth of your own being you can find all you need.

From the safety of your inner universe you can wonder for a moment at the similarity of your body, with its billions of cells, responding at this moment to the healing needs of your body, to the trillions of spheres in the universe. We all wonder about inner and outer space, about what is us and what is universal. We are aware of the mystery, of the creation and re-creation which is constant in inner and outer space. We wonder at the limitless, ungraspable number of cells and planets, satellites and meteors.

Somewhere in this mystery there was a young
planet, fertile, vigorous and curious. The little
planet was experimenting with all the things it
could grow on its surface and was intrigued by
the complexity of its tunnels, caves, volcanoes
and forests. It was trusting and enjoyed the
proximity of other planets.

Then one day a fiery planet loomed close, too
close, out of orbit, until the little planet felt the
force of its gravity and the heat of its surface.
When the invading planet was within range, the
little planet saw that it bore a load of waste that
was both toxic and explosive. The load of waste
crashed onto the surface of the little planet and
the invader continued into deep space.

The little planet felt the pain as its hills became
volcanoes, its lakes boiled, meadows cracked,
forests blackened and sunny beaches darkened.
There were explosions, fires, swamps and then
desolation. Time crusted over the surface, but
underneath, in the caverns, lava swirled.

The little planet broke away from its system
and travelled through space. Sometimes meteors
crashed into it. It had no sense of the future,
only of the past and of loss.

One day the little planet reached a light galaxy
where it felt safe to fall into orbit. It watered
its parched land from its swamps, its chasms
became valleys and its shattered mountains became
exotic islands. Fish grew bizarrely beautiful, trees
thrust into intricate shapes, blossoms adapted into
huge perfumed blooms unlike any other in the

universe. Crystalline rocks shone their wild colours
back to the sun and the animals, tempered by
courage and suffering, became gentle and revered
the planet.

As the planet explored its newness and change and
gloried in what it had become, it became aware of
a dark planet approaching. It knew this dark planet.
But where it had once felt dread, it now felt its
caverns and mountains roar in response to threat.
From its core it gathered up the polluted waste
and with the force of all its volcanoes shot the
poison out of its atmosphere, returning it to the
dark planet from whence it came.

The little planet watched the big planet as it
retreated into the blackness, away from the suns.
It took stock of its land and seascapes. They were
changed, enhanced, unique and responsive. In its
core was fire and strength. Finally it was aware
that all the material it had gathered on its
journey had increased its volume. It was no
longer a vulnerable *little* planet. It knew its inner
resources could overcome attack, that it could
transform, adapt and grow, that its surface and
its interior core worked silently and mysteriously
together to protect and to re-create.

4

Using Your Mind's Resources

Our Beginnings

Sex with children, ritual sacrifice, burning and cauterizing in the name of religion have all been accepted parts of societies' cultures in the past. They are becoming increasingly repugnant to us. Rape is still an intrinsic part of territorial war, but, as with child abuse, it is no longer given societal approval.

Possibly more people in history have been sexually molested than have not. Millions of children were tortured in the Inquisition alone. As all cannot have died as the result of their experiences, they must have found the inner resources to continue and contribute to the relay race which has been human progress.

Carl Jung, the innovative Swiss explorer of the mind, introduced the notion of the 'collective unconscious'; a reservoir of human experience in which is stored our learning over the millennia. When you consider the billions who, throughout history, have conquered the devastation of rape, you can begin to realize the vast resources available to you in your own mind, just waiting to be tapped.

Our genes have travelled through our violent, savage history, but they carry the code which can allow us, as individuals as well as a species, to evolve into stronger, more aware creatures who can decide what we feel and what we do.

Using Trauma to Build Strength

When trauma is incorporated into our reservoir of experience, it becomes a resource; a wise friend instead of an enemy. Throughout the ages religious figures have used the overcoming of pain as a means to develop mind power and universal understanding. Few of us would volunteer for that, but we may as well use the pain we have, especially as we didn't choose it!

If a radio is damaged but continues to work intermittently, we need to look inside and learn how it works if we are to put it right. Likewise, when we want to mend our mind, we have to learn how it works. The following explanations of how the mind works are known as 'constructs', or tools for working with the mind.

PROCESSING TRAUMA

We are as different from each other mentally as we are physically. So what matters is not how terrible our experiences seem to others, but how we feel about them ourselves.

Think of experience as mind food. Good food is easily digested. It integrates with our body and becomes part of us, building strength and health. All experience nourishes us, if we can digest it. Traumatic experience is hard to digest. Like bad food, it can prevent the intake of other nourishment.

Our mind's digestive system starts with arousal. A stimulus causes us to react. We take action, we conclude the action and we return to neutral. The doorbell rings, we answer it, we sign for a parcel and go and sit down again. The experience is digested. But some experiences are less easy to digest.

Imagine you are white. You are walking down the road with a black friend when a racist shouts out an offensive remark. You are outraged, embarrassed, apologetic. Your feelings will not settle, but you dare not tackle the racist and so the experience has no conclusion. It cannot be digested. The next day you see your small daughter throw her black doll downstairs. You are furious and your anger spills out inappropriately. Your unconscious mind was trying to process the incident with the racist, so it grabbed the incident with the doll as a means of expressing the emotion still in the mind's digestive tract.

This is an example of how severe trauma can get stuck between reaction and conclusion. When it does, we need to give it a bit of help, working with it until it is digestible. Once 'digested', even terrible experiences can be remembered without generating painful feelings or controlling our behaviour.

John

Sexually abused by his mother, John survived in his dysfunctional family by developing his imagination as an escape mechanism. He was isolated at school and had a poor academic record. When John was 32 he had a 'breakdown' after his mother's suicide, but was fortunate enough to find a psychiatric team which was trained in sexual abuse. He worked vigorously on his own recovery and in so doing learned a great deal about CSA using this knowledge as the basis for a thesis which eventually earned him a degree.

John then turned to writing - which allowed him to use his super-imagination and life experience - and wrote a TV play based on his childhood, which had a positive ending. Writing the play and watching his childhood re-enacted was therapeutic. John is now a professional screenwriter.

Healing the Mind with Imagery

The use of imagery in healing is powerful because it is natural to our species. Our ancestors knew how to use imagery to change their feelings and they knew how to use their feelings to change events. Before a hunt prehistoric men would draw themselves bringing down their prey. They rehearsed success and were confident they would achieve it. Today we acknowledge that a positive state of mind contributes to success.

Our ancestors also made 'god' figures, which they focused on as they prayed for their needs to be met. We now know that focusing on our healing and believing it possible can facilitate recovery, because the unconscious mind makes little distinction between real and imagined experience. Today we call this technique 'visualization' and it is widely used, with sometimes startling results.

When we are children we use the theatre of our imagination: bullied children create elaborate fantasies of getting even; hated teachers are pushed into sewers; loved teachers are rescued from burning buildings. Lonely children have imaginary friends who help them to learn about sharing and being with other people. Similarly, if we are controlled by traumatic memories, we can disempower them with the help of our imagination.

Ellen

Ellen's childhood lacked all but bodily nourishment. CSA and rape left her unable to look at or touch her own body. She wore men's work clothes and had not bathed for over a decade. Clearly, if she was to tackle her social isolation, bathing was a priority task.

Ellen consulted her imagination and found the easiest place for her to bathe was in a field, alone on a remote island. She needed warm water under a willow tree and flowers in her bath water. She had all that — in her imagination — assisted by *a tape of waves and sea birds, as well as the perfume of tropical flowers. After several 'mind baths' she was able to face the real thing.*

As she challenged her 'cage of can'ts' Ellen's self-image changed, as did her feelings and behaviour. Each success empowered her to face the next challenge and she has now grown into an amusing, warm and elegant woman. It has taken time. Ellen did not start until her forties, but, as she would say, it was change versus more of the same. No contest!

If imagination is augmented by sensory detail, the prosthetic memory is stronger. It is easier to imagine being in a garden if there is real birdsong and smells of grass and flowers.

HOW DOES IT WORK?

Our memory organizes itself in clusters. For instance, each new thing we learn about steam trains will find its way to the 'steam-train' cluster. The more often a cluster is accessed, the quicker its contents are made available. We can even add positive imaginings to our 'traumatic events' cluster so that when it is activated it not only makes available the old feelings but also the positive feelings generated by new therapeutic memories. Eventually, when the pleasant emotions outweigh the unpleasant, the feelings generated by the bad memories will become disempowered and there will be memory without distress.

SCULPTING YOUR BRAIN

Research has shown that the brain builds new systems to cope with our changing needs. For instance, when we learn something new, like driving, cell groups form which hold our new skill. Before long we are driving without having to search our memory and driving feels easy as the new memory chain takes over. Our healing programme is based on taking control of our brain formations.

Shifting Realities

If we pack all our luggage in one bag it can be too heavy to lift. If we divide it between three or four bags, it is possible to distribute the weight so that we can carry it. The human mind works in much the same way.

Even those of us who grew up in loving families encounter some difficulties in childhood which need to be handled by our mind – we may not be as tall as we would like, a beloved uncle may die, we may feel less important than a brother or sister. Conversely, in sexually abusive homes there can be good times, kindness from the abuser, or fun at Christmas. Children respond to kindness and some abusers are adept at giving just enough to keep the child sufficiently needy to be compliant. The abused child learns that it is permissible to speak of the kindness of the carer and it is permissible to speak of eating. The child also learns that what the carer does sexually is not acceptable and, like bowel movements, cannot be spoken about. The child learns the difference. Those who have mainly happy childhoods have similar but less extreme adjustments to make.

It is difficult to hold two conflicting truths at the same time, so our minds keep them in different compartments. Children can happily watch the video of *Babe* while eating a ham sandwich. The pleasure in the food is contained in one truth, the death and suffering of the pig in another.

Moving from one reality to another, abused children experience huge mood swings as different aspects of their personalities manifest in response. The part that experienced kindness can feel optimistic and interact with others. The abused part feels hopeless and mistrustful. In adulthood these alternating realities and resultant severe mood swings can lead to broken relationships, lost jobs and deep depression. Yet by learning how to use the mind's resources, these disadvantages can be overcome.

5

Survival Responses

WHEN WE ARE CHILDREN we develop two mind compartments to cope with conflicting feelings. These can be called the *Victim* state and the *Aggressor* state. These V and A states coexist with the healthy, non-submissive, non-aggressive state we can call the *Integrated* or I state.

In our distant past, when our brains formed in response to our survival needs, we needed to be able to function in one of two ways. When caught by a predator, our choice was: fight or surrender.

When we are attacked we need our brains to produce the chemicals to enhance physical strength and fight back. When we become fighters we are in our A state.

When we cannot escape physically we need to escape mentally. 'Trance' is a state in which we focus on our inner world, with diminished reactions to what is going on around us. Shock can be said to be a form of trance. As many accident victims know, it can be a considerable time before pain from injuries is felt. When escape is impossible, pain and fear have no biological advantage. We become passive. We are in our V state. These mind states enable us to cope with danger and defeat.

Traumatised children are apt to develop exaggerated V and A states, which may dominate until inner conflicts can be resolved. These states should be respected for their role in keeping the personality functioning until such time as the I state can dominate.

The Victim State

The Victim or V state contains learned helplessness and depression. Rape can bring the V state to the fore, as can CSA.

What we believe about our Self is largely based on how adults reacted to us in our first seven years. If adults show a young child he is not valued, the child will feel worthless and his behaviour will reflect this.

Starting school is likely to compound the child's problems. Schoolchildren can be cruel and traumatised children at school are 'different'. 'You are different' easily becomes 'We don't like you', which the child experiences as 'I am not likeable, I am not normal, I am ugly, there is something terribly wrong with me'. Trying to cope with the secrets and the turmoil of a dysfunctional home can leave a sexually abused child in no condition to learn at school. As a result the label 'stupid' is too often added to the list, and 'I can't' precedes many of the child's beliefs. The tension in his body may turn into acne, bad digestion, wetting or other nervous habits. And so the inexorable cycle - belief determining behaviour, behaviour bringing rejection, rejection spawning helplessness - continues. The child develops a personality part to contain his sense of failure - the V state.

When our childhood has not provided us with the experiences needed for emotional well-being, it is easy for us to look on others as 'adults' who can and should take care of us. Life disasters elicit sympathy and sympathy can become a substitute for friendship. When other people weary of this unequal liaison the V state feels betrayed yet again. By now body language expresses our vulnerable feelings and abusive people respond to vulnerability. So the cycle continues.

To those whose V state dominates, other people seem to

have an 'X' factor which accesses worlds permanently closed to them - worlds full of fun, friends, love and success.

The Aggressor State

The Aggressor or A state contains power, anger and self-loathing.

Children learn that expressing the anger they feel can bring disapproval or punishment. When a child fears expressing anger she represses it, stuffing it away deep into the mind where it becomes the A state and acts against the rest of the personality.

Like a bodyguard, the A state is fiercely protective. When operating externally it is a formidable warrior; when directed against the Self it is destructive and cruel. It contains anger and power, but it is also the voice that repeats old beliefs again and again in the mind: 'You are stupid'; 'You can't do it'; 'Go on, cut yourself'.

The A state first came into being when the child needed to cope with a hostile world and, like a soldier unaware that the war has ended, it continues to attack. Absence of battle feels abnormal to the A state, so insults are perceived where there are none. Sometimes the nasty remarks or rejections are real, but often they are our own opinion of ourselves projected onto other people so that we experience them as coming from outside ourselves.

The Integrated State

This state, the I state, can be seen as the person we would have been had we grown up in ideal circumstances. Like a seed which is carried along by a glacier, it can remain dormant until its environment changes and it has all the elements it needs to grow to its full potential. In the I state we neither feel hurt nor have the desire to hurt ourselves or others.

Our therapeutic task is to absorb the Victim and the Aggressor into the I state, leaving ourselves with just enough of them to be useful. Our Victim can be useful in allowing us to communicate our feelings in an appropriate setting, while our Aggressor is a great defender in a threatening situation.

Interactive States

When the I state tries to make progress, the A state attacks it. It might even sabotage us by drinking heavily, cheating on a loved partner, choosing abusive partners, and so on. More subtly, it will remain in unacceptable situations because these hold the magnetic elements of the childhood family trap. It uses other people as weapons to hurt the Self.

Jack

Jack grew up with a mother who punished him severely with violence and ridicule. He learned that he was not strong enough to stand up to her, so he expressed his anger by hiding her clothes when she was going out or opening the oven when she was baking.

When Jack started his first job he experienced his workmates' humour as sneering. He felt victimized and would get back at the men by taking longer and longer to complete tasks. The team became increasingly exasperated and sarcastic with Jack. He suffered deeply from the way they excluded him and was aware of 'Jack jokes' going round the office, so he hid vital pieces of equipment. His behaviour jeopardized the firm's income and therefore his colleagues' jobs, but when they tried to reason with him he remained sullen and unresponsive, feeling hurt, until tempers flared.

Unaware of his own complicity, Jack blamed the mysterious 'something' that had been wrong ever since he was abused as a child. Finally he made a suicide attempt.

Later, in therapy, Jack recognized that he was being abusive to his colleagues in order to make them angry.

Being the focus of anger or sex was the only attention he had had as a child. Now his A state had recreated the misery of his childhood and his V state had felt the old unhappiness.

INTEGRATION

When you have validated and expressed your V state's hurt and harnessed your A state's anger, your personality parts will operate as a cooperative team, with your I state in command. Your Self will be able to live in a world which is not safe, not fair, not what you would choose, but the only one you have!

Sarah

Sarah had exercised her V and A states all her life. Her children were 'too strong for her' and her husband was too indolent to apply for social security payments. The family was sent to a Homeless Families' Unit. Sarah experienced bouts of fury with her children and was often involved in pub fights. Eventually she was referred for therapy.

Sarah reinforced her I state, and after some time left her husband and applied for a nursing course. The administrator of the course put a series of obstacles in her way. In the end he told Sarah that he thought she was unlikely to complete the course. Sarah was furious, but this time did not turn her A state on herself. She resisted the V state's 'He can see you are no good' and the A state's 'He can keep his bloody course. Anyway, he's right, I never finish anything.' Instead she used her A state to resolve to complete the course and show the hostile administrator that she could succeed.

Bringing your V, A and I States to Life

Drawing or modelling your personality parts makes them easy and fun to work with. You can become a detective, out-witting your A state as it tries to sabotage your programme;

you can become a clinician to your timorous V state, knowing when to sympathize and when to be firm. (Jack chose to represent his V state as a cowed and starving stray dog.) Your I state will become stronger as it gains confidence in parenting your V and A states and will find it can transfer these skills to encounters with other people.

Janice

As a child Janice was only noticed by her parents when she was ill or crying, and so she learned that misery and sickness brought the nearest thing to love she had experienced. As an adult, Janice developed one illness after another. Her illnesses caused her to fail at school, in her work and as a parent, and her house looked like a representation of herself — neglected and ailing. Her Victim had taken control of her life.

One day she amazed her neighbours by painting the words 'I am not a poor thing' on her outside wall. The next day she set to work to paint out the words and carried on to paint the whole exterior. She began to enjoy praise as much as she had once enjoyed sympathy. She had extended her feelings about herself to her neglected house, experienced empathy for it, met its needs and changed its very being. By tending a representation of her own Victim she learned to use her V state creatively.

Think of when you have felt helpless and depressed, when you have been in your V state. Draw that 'you' in your book, selecting your colours to reflect the feelings you experienced. You can choose to represent your V state as it was when you were a child, or you can choose to see it as you are now. Alternatively it can be symbolic, like Jack's stray dog. Whichever you choose, your healing must be appropriate to the way you were when you were hurt so that it is compatible with the distressing memories in your brain.

Spend a few minutes looking at your drawing. In your book, write to your V state, thanking it for the service it has done you. This is important because you must avoid allowing your A state to criticize any part of you. Tell your V state that you want it to share the balance of your I state and the courage of your A state. Sympathize with the way it has felt. Validate the positive things it does, like empathizing with others who are hurt and letting you know when you are vulnerable.

Now think of the times when you told yourself you were no good, useless, stupid or ugly, or you hurt yourself or your things, sabotaged relationships or jobs. Draw your A state and write to it. Honour its strength and validate its anger. Ask it to defend your I state and to strengthen your V state.

WORKING WITH CHILDHOOD TRAUMA
If you are working with childhood trauma and choose to represent your A and V states as they were when you were as a child, it is important that you write as if to a child.

Isabel

Isabel is a sophisticated and glamorous adult who used to intellectualize her childhood abuse by an elderly man. During therapy she returned in her mind to the room where she was abused, once again experiencing herself as a four-year-old child. She found she wanted the police to break in and arrest the abuser. She wanted to be carried to the police cells by a big policeman and to wear his helmet. She wanted to put her tongue out at her abuser. When I asked if there was anything else she wanted, she nodded, looking shy. 'What do you want?' She looked up over her hand. 'An ice cream?' she asked hopefully.

Think of a time when you functioned well and felt good. If you hear yourself saying there never was such a time, you are in your V state. Even a minute will do. Draw your I state and write to it. Acknowledge that it has been overwhelmed and promise to put that right. Promise new support from your V and A states. From magazines, cut out pictures of the kind of person you will be and make a poster-sized pastiche for your wall. Make sure you see it often.

Quieten your A state, which is likely to bring doubt into your mind about your ability to become the person you would have been with a trauma-free childhood. This may be your first confrontation with your A state. Use it well - be as strong in your 'no' as you would be with a child wanting to play with piranha fish.

Progress You Can See

Find three glass bowls, if possible in three different colours, perhaps blue, red and green, and some glass nuggets or marbles in the same colours. Each day review your behaviour. When were you in your V state? For each occasion put a blue nugget (or marble) in your Victim bowl. When were you in your A state? Put the appropriate number of red nuggets in the Aggressor bowl. When did you act from your I state? Apportion green marbles to your Integrated state bowl.

This combined visual and feeling exercise will illustrate how much time you spend in each state. Of course, your object is increasingly to feed your I bowl. Review each V and A experience and imagine how your I state would have done it differently.

Teamwork

As we saw earlier, the brain is responsible for releasing waves of chemicals and electrical impulses to aid survival. We need to be strong enough to fight or run away from enemies, so when we experience anger or fear, our brains produce hormones that give us the extra speed and strength we need. If we are unhappy our brains can produce the chemical messengers which cause us to cry – an ancient device which possibly evolved to alert mothers to the needs of babies and can stimulate a built-in nurturing reaction in others. Similarly, the unwanted feelings your ordeal has left you with have been created by your brain to help you survive.

All that you need for your recovery lies in the amazing brain which runs your personal laboratory. It pumps your heart, it breathes for you, makes up therapeutic dramas for you to dream and stores libraries of memories. However, evolution is an opportunistic designer, building on to what it has already created, as it is unable to start again. As mammals evolved, new brain tissue was added around the old reptilian brain which tops the spinal cord. The rational part of the brain is the outer part, folding over the rest like a thinking cap. This newer, thinking part of the brain is divided into two halves: the right half, which is usually responsible for imagination, is perceptive and creative; the left half is logical and analytic.

Our emotions surge from the old part of the brain, the limbic system, which is passionate, selfish, primitive and, above all, a survivor. The area which is responsible for many of our emotions is known as the amygdala. It is one of the different parts of ourselves housed in the brain, each of which has a vital role to play, although not all share the same priorities and beliefs. Personifying these roles can help to resolve emotional conflict.

Inside the Limbic Cave

Imagine having a primitive part of yourself – a keeper of history, a keeper of passion – that is a creature of your limbic system. Get to know your 'Primitive'. Learn what she has to teach, because she can do much that you think you cannot do. What does she look like? What does she wear? What does she eat? What does she have in her cave? Fire? Wolves?

How does she react to sexual attack? How old is she and how long will she live? She has never looked in a mirror, how does that feel? What is her emotional range - anger, fear, love, hate, anything else? Does she know what guilt feels like? Draw her in your book or make a collage. Write about her. Take your feelings to her to test her reaction. Listen to her counsel. Draw the cave. Visit it in your imagination.Take her a gift.

Polly, an African-American who was raped as a child and has a whimsical sense of fun, calls her Primitive Amy Gdala and sees her as an athlete.

The Invisible I State

Sometimes the I state brings about changes in our behaviour while the V and A states continue as if totally unaware of what is happening. It is therefore essential to look at what we are doing as well as what we are feeling. Sometimes the two seem to be totally at odds, as Maggie's story illustrates.

Maggie

Maggie was seven when her mother left the family home, leaving her in the care of her sexually abusive father. When Maggie's father was sent to prison, Maggie went to live with her grandmother. Her life with her grandmother was a narrow one. Maggie was isolated from other children by her grandmother's fundamentalist religion, which perceived God as punishing and inflexible. Maggie saw herself as a tainted being whose Original Sin had manifested at a very tender age. For her the daunting task of avoiding Hell involved complete obedience and servitude.

Maggie's chance to serve presented itself when her grandmother became housebound. The small house became stuffy and dark. Church members came to hold services in her grandmother's room and the old lady was much in demand to cast out demons. Maggie grew increasingly fearful: where did the demons go when her grandmother had cast them out? Were they still in the house? Maggie began to see demons in the shadows and dared not stop praying.

When Maggie was 17 she found her grandmother dead. The church officials demanded that someone watch over the body for two days — that someone was mostly Maggie, who was now thin and nervous and could not imagine what her future might hold.

Maggie's grandmother left her house and savings to the church. She also left Maggie a message urging her to trust that God would provide for her. At this point Maggie started to beat herself regularly, both for her Original Sin and her doubts that her grandmother's God would indeed provide. However, one of the church officials comforted her with extra readings of biblical texts and had sex with her. When Maggie seemed to become emotionally demanding, he found her a live-in job looking after a disabled woman in another county.

Maggie worked day and night in her new job until she eventually developed colitis and was hospitalized. In hospital she struck up an unlikely friendship with Susan, a young woman who had had an abortion. The two shared food treats, watched TV and read Susan's magazines.

Maggie secretly kept up with her new friend after she returned to her job. She also took up her doctor's offer of counselling, which revealed her sexual abuse. She seemed untouched by the anti-depressants prescribed for her and repeatedly told her counsellor that she wanted to die but was too afraid of Hell to kill herself.

At the same time Maggie realized that her small salary had mounted up over the years until she now had several thousand pounds. When Susan told her how much she needed to get away from her husband, Maggie began to take a day off each week. She found a modest house and put down a deposit. Susan moved into the house and paid Maggie rent. Maggie faced her employer and took two nights off a week, but *her employer did not like the new Maggie and sacked her.*

Maggie quickly found work as a care assistant, but she hated it and became even more depressed. To try to shift the depression she went to Spanish dancing classes, for which she found she had talent. Another student invited Maggie to his liberal church and she became aware of alternative beliefs which offered a kind God who was not out to punish her. Susan took her out shopping and gradually Maggie's clothes became more normal for her age group.

Within 18 months Maggie had freed herself from her domineering employer, found a good friend and bought a house. She had also begun to modify her religious beliefs, was earning a better wage and had changed her image.

Maggie experienced these changes as a series of stresses and disasters. When her depression lifted, however, she realized that an invisible part of herself had changed her life completely and that she was now in a position where she had choices and opportunities and could thrive.

Maggie's I state had snatched every opportunity to get her into a situation where she could heal, even though Maggie could not let go of her A state, composed as it was of all she had been taught — that she was bad, that she must serve and that her life on Earth was controlled by a harsh being of infinite power. There had been times when she was on the brink of losing her tenuous hold on reality, yet she grabbed her chance of entering a fuller, happier life through Susan when she could have been expected to recoil from this 'sinner' who had had an abortion.

The invisible I state operates under many names — the 'still quiet voice' and 'intuition' being but two of them. Just as the A state works in the unconscious without our being aware of it, so does the I state, so while we attend to the mundane chores of daily life there are extraordinary battles going on unobserved in our minds as well as our bodies.

Working With Your Team

As you progress, try taking your feelings to your group of selves – your Primitive, your Aggressor and your Victim selves – which together make you, or your I state. Although these personality parts are common to us all, yours arise from your own experience. They are your unique team of personality parts and each has a useful role to play.

What is your team like together? Whatever kind of fiction you enjoy, see your team as characters in that setting – a family, an army unit, a team of Victorian explorers have all been used. If you are a sci-fi enthusiast, you could turn them into the crew of a space vessel and so on. Some people have modelled their parts and used the models as if in a role-playing board game; others have drawn them onto cards. Using the characters in this way allows you to consult your whole team and thus use all your resources when confronting a challenge or implementing changes in yourself. Perhaps most important of all, it is a fun way of working.

The following is an extract from a piece of work done by Rob, who had not been out socially since his rape.

ROB: **Can I cope with the club tonight?**

AGGRESSOR: **Of course you can't. You're a coward. I can, though.**

PRIMITIVE: **Cowards die before they are ten. You must go, you must bond with the tribe. Wait till many gather and it is dark. Stay alert and listen to the drumming, it will give you courage. There is no more time to waste. Life is soon over. I know how to recover from rape. My immediate ancestors recovered. If they had not been able to function after rape they would have died. We are born from a long line of survivors.**

VICTIM: **I can't. It is not over for me.**

I STATE: **Then stay inside me and Primitive and Aggressor, we'll cope with this one.**

Rob got in touch with all aspects of himself. He saw his emotional confusion spread out in a manageable format and gave attention to each conflicting urge so that no part of him could take him unawares. Knowing the different parts of himself allowed him to summon up their images when he needed to use them. Of course, he knew he was working with characters that had no life beyond his imagination, but he was able to use the same facility he had had as a child when he made a cardboard box into a boat on the sea of the living-room carpet.

6

Understanding Your Self

THIS CHAPTER IS primarily for those who were sexually abused as children.

Understanding Why You Do the Things You Do

WHY DO I SLEEP AROUND WHEN I DON'T WANT TO?
When you were a child sex may have been associated with false closeness and intimacy. Now you may be experiencing a desperate loneliness which drives you to search constantly for a fulfilment you cannot name. This search may lead you into a sad series of sexual encounters which are neither erotic nor loving, with each one leaving you more desperate and lonely.

A child who is abused by close family members is effectively an orphan. In most species, the young who lose their parents have a survival mechanism which drives them to try to attract other adults to take care of them. Maybe you are acting from this ancient drive.

How can you not do it? Know that this robotic behaviour can be dismantled. How will you go about dismantling it? Each time you resist it you are wiping out a bit more of your old pattern.

WHY DO I CHOOSE PARTNERS TO ABUSE MYSELF WITH?
As we seek to recreate the conditions of our childhood, so we seek aspects of our parents in our partners. How many times have we heard someone say to his partner, 'You sound just like my mother'? This is not serendipity, but unconscious choice. If our childhood was traumatic, we may choose partners to beat us up, to reject and humiliate us with their unfaithfulness, to use our financial resources, to embarrass us and to leave us. We can use them to say aloud the cruel things we whisper to ourselves.

The trick is to choose the I state of your parent and not the V or A state.

SELF-STARVATION
For a victim of sexual abuse the refusal to eat often starts with a sense of being 'bad'. In our image-conscious society 'bad' easily becomes 'unacceptable' and 'unacceptable' becomes 'ugly'. To many people, 'fat' also means 'ugly'. This distortion is projected onto the person in the mirror and overrides all other information. Then magic enters our thinking. Just like small children who think to themselves, 'If I don't tread on the cracks in the pavement, I'll get my maths right,' so we think, 'If fat can be conquered, then life will be different.'

Starvation creates a body chemistry which distances anguish and produces a light-headedness not dissimilar to some drug-induced states. This effect has been used since biblical times by mystics who fasted and had visions.

Self-starvation may also be an expression of feeling like a child. Children are small, have no breasts and do not menstruate. Similarly, when a woman starves herself her breasts disappear, menstruation ceases and she becomes small. Advanced starvation means being cared for like a child, spoon-fed and lifted. Some men also starve themselves, but far fewer than women.

Also, when a child is forced to practise fellatio and

loathes it, she will sometimes transfer the need to keep genitals out of the mouth to other substances. For instance, food that is reminiscent of ejaculate is rejected. Refusing to eat porridge or fish can give the feeling of having some control and later this taboo can be extended to all food. Some children forced to swallow ejaculate vomit afterwards. Perhaps this is replayed in the 'binge and throw up' syndrome. Vomiting into containers and hiding it is reminiscent of hiding secrets in childhood.

SELF-CUTTING AND BURNING

Sometimes self-loathing, anger or shame can become so intense that they are harder to bear than physical pain. When this happens, physical pain itself can seem to alleviate the feelings, because the brain laboratory reacts to pain by releasing 'feel good' chemicals. We each have different amounts of these chemicals and those whose brains release large amounts of these morphine-like substances can become psychologically dependent on them.

When we feel shame, the A state says accusingly, 'You have just said/done something so stupid I want to hurt/obliterate you.' The attack creates internal chaos and a loss of contact with a large part of the Self. Like damaged robots, we pace the room compulsively and purposelessly, making random movements, full of destructive energy for which there is no outlet.

Painful self-harm may be the restoration of a lost sense of control. A slap across the face of a hysterical person will restore calm. Electro-convulsive therapy (ECT) can relieve deep depression (although no one knows quite how). Pain has also been used as a means of restoring self-acceptance for centuries by religious penitents and so lies deep in our group memory. Knowing that we can bear pain, or that we have the courage to cut or beat ourselves can restore some order to the chaos. It can also give us a sense of achievement.

Practical Work

Symptoms

Turn back to the symptoms listed on pages 32–4. Mark each one with a V or an A. It doesn't matter whether you behave in this way or not. Copy your own symptoms into your book, dividing them into:

1 *those that will change as you learn to like and respect yourself*

2 *those you want to keep*

For instance, you may want to keep your nurturing job but lose your unreasonable outbursts of anger.

Inappropriate Anger

Who are you really angry with when you blast off at someone who is close to you? Write down what you say to your partner in anger. Try saying it to a photograph or drawing of your carers and abusers as they were when you were a child. Go through the list of the people who damaged you until you find a match that 'feels' right – probably your rapist, abuser or parent. Now express your anger to the picture of the person it fits.

Having No Sexual Feelings

CHILD SEXUAL ABUSE
Sometimes we can learn more effectively by teaching than by being taught. Explain to a drawing of your I state child that flowers are a plant's sexual organs. Write about sex as an expression of love and trust, of bodies as amazing sensory receptors, and of the pure ecstasy of orgasm.

When you have your first sexual fantasies, cherish them – provided, of course, that they are not cruel and do not include children or reinforce an abuse/abuser blueprint – and, as children do, replay them as you touch yourself.

ADULT SEXUAL ABUSE

Imagine a small island or planet which is only habited by you. Make your new home wonderful by gradually introducing all the things you enjoy. Make the climate just right and when it is, design your house. No one can reach your island or planet without your permission.

When you have drawn, written about or modelled your new home, gradually introduce the people you want to be there with you. Design one to love. Imagine just lying with this special person. As time passes you will probably want to progress to more intimate touching. When sex feels comfortable in your imagination, you are ready to heal.

Not Being Able to Let Go of the Abuser

Those who have not been lonely and abused children are apt to view the relationship between abuser and abused in black and white: the abused is expected to feel anger and resentment and expel the abuser from her life. But often this is not what she wants.

When seduction has been the method used by the abuser to gain access to a vulnerable child, the attachment can be strong. The attention may have been the nearest thing to love the child knew. If the relationship survives into adulthood, trading it in to meet the expectations of helpers is hard to do – as hard as relinquishing the escape provided by drugs. Attachment dies hard and the relationship may continue until the abused person feels sufficiently secure in other relationships.

If the abuser receives treatment and genuinely regrets and understands what has happened, a new way of relating is occasionally possible. Sometimes this happens when a parent is arrested and treated for child abuse and rejoins the family under supervision. Without this, if the relationship continues, the abused person is apt to collude with the abuser's lie that it was 'all right really'.

Stockholm Syndrome

Those who are abused repeatedly in a relationship can bond to their rapist by a phenomenon known as 'Stockholm Syndrome' – an emotional dependence on, and obsession with, the abuser which the victim forms as a means of enduring the situation. Once formed, this bond is hard to break.

With or without rape, it seems that it is the power that is crucial. In the USA in the 1970s high-society rich girl Patty Hearst was kidnapped by the 'Symbionese Liberation Army' and bonded so tightly with her kidnappers that some months later she was robbing a bank with them.

Stockholm Syndrome can cause the victim to trivialize the most horrific rape. For some bonded victims it feels worse to lose the attention of the rapist than to continue to be used sexually.

Shunning Children

Adults who, when they were little, felt that they were unpleasant and unwelcome often have difficulties in responding to children. For them, the smells and sounds of childhood can activate feelings of shame or fear. A child who learns he is not lovable also learns, in child logic, that children are not lovable, yet society needs us to love children and the survival of our species depends upon it. There is therefore an inference that, if we do not love children, we are bad people. In some adults this can add to an already heavy guilt load.

A dislike or fear of children often disappears with personal healing and familiarity, although some people have had to learn to see children as animals before being able to relate to them properly as children. After a while this ploy usually becomes unnecessary.

It is important to understand that discomfort around children is not the same thing as wishing them harm. It is a form of self-loathing, the legacy of a miserable childhood, and no more a legitimate cause of shame than a fear of sex.

7

Childhood Memories

'I Can't Remember'

Some people are sexually traumatized but have no memory of having been abused. For as long as they can remember they have believed alternately that they were abused and that they were 'making it up'. They feel fraudulent and unable to trust their own perceptions, but, as we have already seen, the psyche copes with trauma by creating alternating realities.

When in the 'I'm making it up' reality such people feel as if they have no 'right' to their feelings and possibly use their A state to punish themselves for being 'mad' or attention seeking. When in the 'certain it happened' reality they feel chaotic. There is a dream-like feeling of being on the brink of remembering something that has been temporarily forgotten. Rage, fear and self-loathing vie for control. Certain sights, words or smells associated with sex can trigger unpleasant feelings in the body. Some people describe these feelings as pains, others screw up their limbs and grimace as if chewing slugs.

Often there is a sense of mistrust of parents, or those who were in a parental role, and when parents engender feelings of sexual disturbance it can seem that they are the obvious suspects.

Partners can seem to 'turn into' someone else during sex, replaced by the sight, and sometimes the smell, of a powerful person from the past. This momentary delusion can be very frightening and those who have it sometimes fear for their sanity if they do not understand why it happens. These transformations during love-making can be particularly destructive to a relationship. No one wants to be pushed away and told that their partner thought they were their mother! This may happen because the sexual act 'wires into' a childhood trauma. The stimulated brain may produce the visual flashback in an attempt to resolve the trauma or because the memories are associated in the brain's sex cluster.

Some people have parents who fit the abusive family profile – one dominant parent with a benign public face and a malign private face and one compliant, victim-like parent. Often siblings have emotional and social difficulties. Sometimes each sibling has conflicting memories of early family life, as if each grew up in a different family. This indicates that each child 'edited' what was happening to create a reality in which he could have some of his needs met. Sometimes each sibling will unconsciously select one parent to be the good one and one to be the bad one, just pushing out of consciousness whatever does not fit the scenario. When siblings select different 'good' parents, their conflicting views challenge each other's reality and sad family splits can occur.

One or both parents may have had mental health problems which have created a family environment sufficiently unhealthy to cause their children emotional difficulties without sexual abuse having been a factor. This is even more confusing, because dysfunctional families provide an ideal environment for sexual abuse to flourish.

Some people who believe they have amnesia of sexual abuse have not actually been abused. They feel the cause of their symptoms must be dramatic and horrific because their distress is so great and the unconscious seizes upon sexual abuse because it meets the conscious demand for a cause as dreadful as their feelings. However, ongoing emotional pain can be caused by early emotional deprivation.

Also, the effects on girls of growing up with absent or rejecting fathers can be much the same as sexual abuse. Not being touched (safely) as a child can yield results similar to those of being inappropriately touched. The symptoms of emotional, physical and sexual abuse are very similar in all but sexual matters.

Some people may have been abused sexually at a time when their brains were not sufficiently developed to be capable of making coherent memories but were still able to experience extreme emotion. It is possible to remember in ways not fully explained but well established.

Others, when abused as older children, have coped with their confusion and distress by forgetting the experience or, to put it another way, allowing one of their realities to dominate or suppress the others. Amnesia is the ultimate escape from reality.

Others really do remember, but fear admitting that their memories are real. It can seem as if admitting abuse can rob them of their 'normal' Self, as if once abuse is admitted one becomes 'abnormal'. The media often portray people who have been abused as disturbed or dangerous, ignoring the millions who have managed the symptoms of their abuse while living useful and full lives. 'Remembering' can also threaten relationships with parents suspected of abuse, parents who, despite everything, are often loved.

Denying a conviction that you have been abused can also seem like a betrayal of yourself and a relinquishing of trust in your perception of reality. Unable to resolve the dilemma, some people opt for alternating realities as a means of avoiding the consequences of either. The trouble with alternating realities is that they are very confusing and can even make you question your own sanity.

The Use of Hypnosis in Regaining Memories

Those who believe they have amnesia of abuse often believe that if they could just remember what happened to them they would at least not feel 'crazy' because they would have one reality. This desire to know the truth has understandably led many to seek it through hypnosis.

Usually there is no way of telling whether an early memory 'regained' under hypnosis is real, though occasionally it has been possible to verify retrieved memories. However, the nature of memory is little understood. As any policeman will tell you, people witnessing the same event remember it very differently. As scientific research has shown, people who have lost the parts of the brain which hold certain memories have still had recall. It is also possible to implant false memories which are then experienced as real. All this means that the certainty of 'knowing' in many cases is impossible.

Some therapists in the USA who claim to have helped their clients 'regain' memories of sexual abuse have encouraged them to seek financial compensation from their supposed abusers. This has led to the 'False Memory Syndrome' controversy, where those accused of child abuse defend themselves by claiming that the therapist has implanted the client's memories of abuse. This has caused a great deal of mistrust and has resulted in the public recoiling from what is a genuine and agonising situation - which makes it even more difficult for people who cannot remember to feel that their experiences are valid.

Those who have been deeply hurt by others may feel unconsciously that only childhood sexual abuse would bring the odium their abusers deserve. However, there are people who have started out in therapy with a strong and honest conviction that they were abused and then realised during therapy that they were not. Others have begun therapy believing their childhood to have been normal, only to discover that they were abused. This is why it is vital to leave a margin of doubt before stating forgotten abuse as a fact.

Healing Without Your Memory

Coming to terms with not knowing what caused your emotional distress is not easy. It is therefore important to work with the childhood trauma you do remember and not to scorn it, because processing *any* painful material will increase your well-being.

Also, your unconscious is more likely to release suppressed memories to a mind strong enough to handle them. If the memories were suppressed in the first place, it was for your own protection. When you no longer need that protection there will be no need for the memories to be withheld.

It is not necessary to regain memory in order to change the way you feel. Many people are now thriving who were once governed by feelings for which they have never known the cause.

The fear of regaining memories of painful events can sometimes help to prevent their recovery. Yet often the recovery is not painful at all.

Lisa

Lisa had been in therapy for some time, working through her abuse by her father. She was also building an exciting new life for herself which was taking her from Birmingham to London to give a presentation. She was driving with her dearest friend, who was asking her about her relationship with Harry, her partner. It was an unsatisfactory relationship which Lisa was realizing must end. Lisa's friend asked if sex was the hook that kept her with Harry. 'Could be,' acknowledged Lisa. 'He is a lot like my brother sexually.'

Until that moment she had no conscious memory of her sexual relationship with her brother, but as soon as she heard herself say the word she had access to a flood of memories. The women pulled into a lay-by for a while. Lisa was fascinated by the way events suddenly made sense. She felt no distress, only a certain elation, similar to that of solving a difficult puzzle.

Only six months earlier Lisa would have accessed her V state, felt this 'new' information to be traumatic and have asked for comfort or drunk a bottle of whisky to help her 'cope with it', or manifested her A state and told herself she was to blame. As it was she stayed in her I state. The two friends continued to London and Lisa gave her presentation.

The False Child

We are born with no self-image. We gradually construct one from the reactions of others to us. If adults smile and hug us and are pleased by our presence, we learn that we are a source of pleasure. If adults are irritated by our presence, we believe that there is something wrong with us: anger tells us we are bad; impatience tells us we are unimportant; misery tells us we are depressing. In an abusive family anger and blame are often vented on the youngest members. Sexually abusive families are by definition dysfunctional families which can provide only dysfunctional parenting.

When negative adult reactions cause a young child to experience her Self as bad, she begins to construct a protective psychological shell around the 'bad' Self, at the same time constructing a 'good' Self outside the 'bad' capsule. Only the unconscious remembers the 'bad' Self, and this unconscious memory creates a sense of having a shameful 'something' inside, something too threatening to the child's self-esteem for her to face. The non-existent monstrous inner Self feels too shameful to bring into consciousness.

From the negative reactions of those around young children is born the 'false child', a child built of rejection and the impatience, incompetence, stress, preoccupation or cruelty of others. Like a ghost, this child inhabits the real person until she is exorcized by the understanding of how she came into being. Once the false child has been banished, the adult is free to realize the potential to be the confident person she would have grown into without the abuse.

Paul

Paul often witnessed his drunken mother having sex with men. She spent little time or money on him. He went to school in dirty and inappropriate clothes and the other children made him their group victim, from which Paul learned that he was dirty and laughable, repulsive, unimportant and unlikeable. At school he learned that people are cruel and that he was different; at home he learned that he was valueless and that the most he had to give was his absence.

Sue

Ever since she could remember, Sue had been unwanted by both her parents. One of her earliest memories was of her parents fighting about who was to be 'lumbered' with her. She heard her mother phoning her grandparents to beg them to take her, but they did not want her either. Her mother often told her she hated her and her father rarely used her name, referring to her as 'Stupid'. When asked why she told no one of her beatings and abuse, she said, 'I thought they would say, "Of course they don't want you, of course they beat you, you are so awful, of course your father has sex with you, all fathers do that," and I couldn't bear to hear it.'

The Sanctified Parent

Adults with abuse in their childhood can often form a deep attachment to the non-abusing parent of whom they have only good memories. However, towards the end of therapy, just as it seems that all the basic changes have been made, there can be a last minute revelation about the 'good' parent. (I say 'basic changes' because our psyches are like gardens: there is always weeding and feeding to be done and stuff to be recycled.)

Once the rage against the active abuser has been expressed it can come as a shock to find there is a whole cache of anger for the 'blameless' parent. Questions begin to be asked: 'Why did she not notice there was something wrong?' 'Surely he noticed blood on my underclothes, bruises when I was in the bath?' 'Why was I not able to tell them? My kids would tell me if there was something wrong.' Questions like these can be suppressed by feelings of disloyalty to the sanctified parent, but they will only present themselves again. At some point they must be faced.

CONFRONTING THE SANCTIFIED PARENT

This often means a break, albeit a temporary one, with the 'good' parent while feelings are explored and expressed. Sometimes it is useful to confront a parent, but only if he is young enough to make changes. Challenging an elderly parent who may die in the near future can only harm the challenger, who may suffer guilt and doubt for the rest of her life. Challenging someone who is incapable of giving the reaction the challenger wants can only make things worse.

Older people are often unable to remember the past accurately. Our need to believe that our lives have been successful increases as our life expectancy decreases. We are apt to edit our memories in order to leave our self-regard unsullied. A confrontation of the 'Yes, you did!'/'No, I didn't!' kind only damages both participants, each of whom needs to validate his own reality. Both can be telling the truth as they believe it to be, while violating the truth of the other. This is destabilizing for someone who has just changed his beliefs about the person being challenged.

Many people maintain a very close adult relationship with unsatisfactory parents, upon whom they depend heavily. This relationship can be more important to them than their relationship with their partner or children, because unconsciously they still yearn for the parenting they never had and continually hurt themselves by attempting to get it.

WHY DOES A CHILD SANCTIFY A PARENT?

It is a curse of childhood that our bonding instinct does not discriminate between good and bad parents. Many adults who bonded with bad parents when they were children, remain bound to them in what is probably a poignant attempt to get enough parental love to allow them to be independent.

Adequate parenting is the ladder to maturation. Without it we can only stand at the bottom and act as if we are at the top. In order to keep a foot on the ladder the child needs to feel accepted by at least one person. Maybe the ingenious unconscious creates the illusion of one good parent out of two in order to progress. This takes a great deal of editing and some creativity, but these are just the resources sexually abused children have in abundance.

Amber

Amber was adopted when she was a baby, but her mother tired of the responsibilities of motherhood. She and her lover moved from one area to another when Amber was six, when they stopped sending her to school. When the child's presence at home provoked questions, they locked her in her room with Victorian novels and trained her to be silent when people came to the house.

Eventually the windows in Amber's room were boarded up so that she could not be seen, her meals became irregular and she had only cats and her imagination for company. Sometimes she was made to share a litter tray with the animals and her mother put powder cleaner in the wash basin to make sure she did not use that instead. Once Amber was held under near-boiling water.

This was the life Amber lived for nearly 20 years while her mother lived in a la-la land of drugs and self-aggrandisement. During her rare visits to Amber she would tell her of her lover's unkindness.

Amber was eventually sexually abused by her mother's lover. When her mother found out she threw Amber out into a strange world totally alien to the one she had learnt about in the Victorian books she had been given.

Amber contacted the Samaritans and the first thing she asked for was help to rescue her mother. It was two years before she could relinquish her 'good parent' image of her abusive mother.

Practical Work

Working 'As If'

Remembering is not essential for healing. However, memories are useful because they trigger feelings and it is bad feelings that are the problem. Memories without feelings are no problem.

If a story can trigger feelings, why not use a story when you have no memory of abuse? Throughout history human beings have used stories to express extremes of feeling. Now we have theatre, films, literature and drama for expressing our own emotions through identification with others. Some men cry when their football team loses a game. The death of Diana, Princess of Wales, released floods of grief in millions of people who had never met her. Even the death of characters in soap operas has allowed people to express genuine sorrow.

If you already have a scenario which fits your feelings but do not know whether it is true, you can use this scenario to heal your feelings while suspending your need to believe whether it is true or not. You can even consciously make up a story of abuse that fits your feelings and work with it *as if* it were true, while knowing that it is fiction.

No Memory of Abuse

Write a story which includes all that you fear may have happened to you. Make simple illustrations. Monitor your feelings as you write, noting them in the margin.

When you have finished, choose the situations which created the strongest feelings when you were writing, then rate them in order of strength. Write your feelings in your book as they were experienced by the child in the story.

Speak your feelings into your tape recorder, adding the comforting words you would have wanted to hear as the child. Play them back to yourself until the recording no longer distresses you.

Continue until you can use all the therapies in this book which would be suitable for the child in your story.

Remember that when you have healed your feelings the need to know whether you were really abused will probably have diminished.

Healing the False Child

Draw yourself as a child. If you like the child, you have drawn the real child. If you feel hostile to the child, you have drawn the false child. Discover what this self-perception consisted of and make a list – for instance, 'You are my father's drink problem', 'You are my mother's misery and anger', 'You are my uncle's perversion.'

It can be both dramatic and powerful to have a ceremony of farewell to the child who never was. Some people have burned their 'false child' drawings, feeling that the child was being returned to thin air from whence it came. What would you like to do?

8

Understanding Your Darkest Fears

The Darkest Fears of Pre-Sexualized People

WILL I BECOME A CHILD ABUSER?

If you have been abused it does not mean that you will have a sexual response to children. If you have never had a sexual impulse towards a child as an adult, it is unlikely that you will now.

If you are one of the few who does have an occasional, mild sexual response to children that you have never considered acting upon, there is no reason to believe that these urges will strengthen or become more frequent. Nonetheless, the existence of such feelings in those who revile them can cause terror. Some people shun children in order to avoid the feelings which can seem to justify self-loathing.

Our first sexually arousing experience can become the model for all that follow. Sexual drives coexist with other drives, such as the drive to be acceptable to others or to protect the young of our species. We all have negative drives, such as violence, inappropriate sexual desire and the urge to take what we want, but we mostly overcome them. Having an urge to kill someone is not the same as committing murder.

Inappropriate sexual urges are more powerful when we are disabled by fear. Fear thrives in ignorance and the way to overcome ignorance is to understand where our fear comes from.

WHY DO I HAVE THESE FEELINGS?

So, why should someone who was sexually abused as a child be aroused by children? It may be that when your own abuser was aroused, she produced certain chemicals which transmit sexual arousal from one person to another. Children are understandably confused when they experience disgust, fear and arousal all at the same time. Later on in life, certain triggers may reproduce similar confusion.

The trance-like state experienced by a child during abuse is ideal for the feelings of the abuser to be imprinted, just as the instructions of a hypnotist are absorbed by a subject in trance. In this way the cocktail of chemical stimuli experienced by children can trigger the release of childhood feelings in adults. In other words, they are the feelings imprinted by your abuser. With courage and practice you can jettison them, or learn to manage them. Becoming erect in the street, being secretly aroused by a best friend's husband, having sexual fantasies about being raped are all common experiences which we do not readily own.

We overcome strong impulses all day and every day. For instance, we can have a full bladder without succumbing to the impulse to empty it in the delicatessen. Sometimes simply admitting that an impulse is there is enough to begin to disassemble it. Sometimes it is not. *Only you know whether you could offend against a child.* The best therapist can only use the data you supply.

If you have any doubt about your ability to overcome your impulses, it is imperative that you work with a sex therapist. If you doubt the wisdom of this, write the story of a future in which you have abused a child. Include the consequences for you and for the child.

Sex therapists work with sexual arousal on a daily basis and come to view it much as a mechanic views the workings of a petrol engine. They will not judge you or experience the 'shock horror' reaction you dread. After all, you have sought their help because you do not want to abuse.

WILL I ALWAYS LOATHE SEX?

As you heal your trauma, so you will climb the maturation ladder. When you reach the emotional age at which sex is appropriate, you are likely to begin to feel sexual urges appropriate to that age.

Most people who have feared and abhorred sex find that when they have done sufficient work their relationships with others have changed dramatically. Almost unnoticed, friendships are made with new people, people very different from previous friends. Happy people are attracted to happy people. So you may find that whereas in the past some unconscious recognition process attracted people with difficulties, now people more at peace with themselves want to know you. This can lead to a trusting relationship with one particular person, which may then lead easily and naturally to sexual expression.

It is usual for young people to experience orgasm through touching their own bodies. Privacy provides the security in which to experiment. Once your mind and body have a safe and trusting sexual partnership it is easier to share sexual pleasure with someone you love and respect.

WILL I BE ABLE TO STOP SABOTAGING MYSELF?

It is easy for us to accept that a child who grows up in a healthy family will try to create a similar family when he becomes adult, or that someone who takes good feelings for granted as a child will consider them normal and regard misery as unacceptable. However, it is more difficult for us to accept that those to whom it was normal to feel bad as children will try to recreate their childhood circumstances in adulthood.

None of us would readily admit that we set ourselves up to fail, to create septic relationships, to distort our body image or to seek abusive friends. While we may understand about salmon, turtles and homing pigeons seeking to return to their place of origin, sometimes at the cost of their lives, we find it hard to accept that we have an unconscious drive to create replicas of our childhood, to return to a *feeling*. Yet it is because of this unconscious drive that children from violent homes are more likely to become violent people or victims of violence, thereby creating an inexorable replay of their original turmoil.

What might you be trying to recreate? Once you know, you can outsmart the part of yourself that sets you up.

Self-sabotage is a battle between the I state, which strives for better things, the V state, which fears change, and the A state, which is in charge of discipline. Self-sabotage is eating a cream cake when you are dieting. It is forgetting the map on a long trip; finding someone you love and then being unfaithful or letting your appearance go; missing the train or forgetting to press 'save' on your computer when you've worked through the night. Self-sabotage is studying hard, then picking a row with your partner hours before the exam. You sit your exam, but your mind is replaying the row and projecting yourself into a lonely and miserable future. When the results come, you have failed. It was just one of those things. Or was it? Did you leave yourself wide open to rejection that morning? Could you have chosen a partner with a vested interest in blocking your progress?

Jane

Sexually abused as a child, Jane was starting again after a series of life disasters. She was doing well at her college course, to which she drove across country late at night in her old banger. Many times, though, she ran out of petrol. Eventually, she was assaulted by a lorry driver in a lay-by. For a while afterwards she felt helpless. No matter how hard she tried these things kept happening to her; other people could go to college, but not her. Her V state ruled her internal logic.

Once again Fate seemed to have dealt Jane a cruel blow. Or had it? Was it not a hidden, aggressive, self-destructive part of her that 'forgot' to buy petrol? The lorry driver was culpable, of course, but could Jane's A state have set her up to return to the familiar despair like a homing-pigeon struggling back to a bad home?

Having gained insight and learned to be on the lookout for her A part, Jane learned to plan her journeys, owned her complicity in making herself vulnerable, expressed her fury with the lorry driver, took him to court, counted having 'caught out' her A state as a victory and got on with her course. She learned that deer need to avoid hounds — simply protesting that hunting is wrong will not keep them safe.

WILL I ALWAYS FEEL COMPELLED TO HAVE SEX WITH WHOEVER WANTS ME?

We have looked at the way in which a trance state is induced in the victim of attack. A situation which has sufficient elements of the original abuse can induce the original state of helplessness. If you learned sexual helplessness, it is not surprising that your V state barters sex for company and what may seem to substitute for affection. As you come to understand the way your childhood shaped you, you can fight the urge to restage your past abuse.

> **There was this hunk. He said he was sure he could talk to me because I looked as if I knew what it is like to be hurt. His wife had thrown him out and he had no money and nowhere to stay. He was already pretty drunk. I said, 'That's tough, mate.' A couple of months ago I'd have moved him in.**

AM I REALLY GAY?

Children who had a same-sex abuser may be driven to restage their trauma with same-sex partners. If gay relationships feel safe and satisfying, then you are likely to be acting from your orientation and not your abuse. If same-sex encounters leave you feeling sullied and miserable, while opposite-gender sex does not, and your sexual fantasies are same-sex, then you may be re-enacting your original trauma and the urge for gay sex is likely to disappear as you heal.

I ENJOYED THE SEX WHEN I WAS A CHILD. DOES THIS MEAN IT WAS MY FAULT?

Children need touch. They do not thrive without it. We are apes and like other apes we are born with a clinging response. We were designed to be carried close to our mothers' bodies and rarely put down. Touch and closeness meant safety and belonging, the difference between life and death. Being touched and held meant being bonded, and that meant food and protection. Not being touched could mean lack of love and abandonment to starvation and predators.

A child has a body whose mouth responds to good tastes and whose genitals respond to gentle touching. She also has an ancient drive to groom and be groomed, for we were once groomed when the tribe was at rest. New to the world, she cannot understand that it is fine to enjoy some things that feel good and not others. Inappropriate touching may feel good and gain approval from abusive adults. Sex, like fire and sharp knives, may sometimes be attractive to children, but it is the responsibility of adults to keep them safe.

WHY WAS I JEALOUS OF MY ABUSED BROTHER?

An older child who is abused pleasurably for the first time is usually carefully groomed by the abuser, who will ensure that he associates touching with treats such as presents and games, and will ease him from one stage of intimacy to the next almost imperceptibly. The child can become psychologically dependent upon the sex and thus upon the abuser.

If the sex is withdrawn, or the abuser's attention transferred to another child, the sense of loss and abandonment can be overwhelming and jealousy follows naturally. Sometimes one child is dropped for a younger one because paedophiles are often fixated on children of a certain age, which may correspond to the age at which they themselves were abused. The 'dumped' child may grow up unconsciously setting up situations which end in rejection, constantly reinforcing the early lesson: 'I get rejected.'

WHEN I WAS LITTLE I USED TO TRY TO HAVE SEX WITH OTHER CHILDREN. DOES THAT MEAN I AM AN ABUSER?
A pre-sexualized child will sometimes involve other children in sexual acts. Adults often react harshly to this, causing the child to believe he is a bad, dirty person other children's parents do not want around. Thus alienated, he begins to build defences, such as cutting off sexual feeling, or obsessive masturbation. (Masturbation – temporarily at least – can blot out some of the loneliness and rage felt by the child.)

These life events can contribute to some people becoming abusers, but they do not make it inevitable. An abuser is not something that you can turn into, like a werewolf.

George

George was five when his mother moved her lover and his two teenaged sons into their squalid high-rise apartment. The boys all slept together in one bed. The big boys dominated and bullied George, whose mother had very little time for him.

Soon the bullying became sexual and George was raped by both boys. Overnight the semen worked like an enema and by the morning George had soiled the bed. His mother made him stand in a corner with a notice round his neck which read: 'I am a dirty little bugger.'

George grew up in the violent atmosphere of his home city and became big and tough. He found his sexual feelings were aroused by small boys and feared that one day he might offend. Consciously or unconsciously — he was never sure which — he put himself in prison to prevent this. He broke into jewellers', he got into fights, causing grievous bodily harm, and he stole loaded trucks.

For 30 years he kept himself mostly behind bars where there were no children. Then at 50, scarred and having had enough of prison, he sought help from an agency which worked with adults who were abused as children. After a stringent course of treatment, George felt ready to live in the community. After all, he had never offended, he was acutely aware of the pain caused by child abuse and his odium for child abusers was in no doubt.

His younger brother had kept in touch while George was in jail. With the support of his therapist, George told his brother the whole truth in a letter explaining why he would not accept an invitation to stay. His brother responded by offering him a cottage with a couple of acres in return for half the produce and some shepherding.

George is still there with his animals and says he is at peace. He and his brother's family have bonded in an almost non-verbal way. George began to spend Christmas with them some years ago and he says he felt no sexual desire for the children. He has no reason to lie. After all, he has done nothing wrong.

The Darkest Fears of Those Who Have Been Raped

PART OF ME RESPONDED SEXUALLY WHILE I WAS BEING RAPED. DOES THIS MEAN I 'ASKED FOR IT'?
What it means is that your body responded automatically to the stimuli you were experiencing and the chemicals

(pheromones) that you were breathing in. You know whether or not you consented to what happened. If you did not, or did so under threat, you were raped. If you said 'no', you were not 'asking for it'. If you are wondering whether your behaviour was enticing until force was applied, only you can answer that. Even if you were enticing and you later said 'no', you were still raped.

If you have doubts about your behaviour, take this opportunity to examine it honestly. If you were risk-taking, is there a self-destructive part of you that might have used the rapist to hurt yourself?

Risk-taking is common in our species. We race cars, we go to war, we bungee jump. Some people say that risk-taking is a search for a natural high, while others claim we are attracted to death just as we are repelled by it. Risk-taking can be a sort of unconscious Russian roulette played by those whose V state feels they need to be punished for some real or imagined transgression. If you find you were risk-taking, it is better to own it now so that you can make informed choices in future.

WILL I EVER WANT SEX AGAIN?

If you enjoyed sex before you were raped, there is no reason why you should not enjoy it again when you have worked through your trauma. In fact you may well iron out some old hang ups as you work, so you may even enjoy it more.

DID MY RAPIST RECOGNIZE 'GAYNESS' WHEN HE CHOSE ME?

Heterosexuals can fear that their same-sex rape was provoked by their latent homosexuality. But a rape is a statement about the rapist, not the one who is raped. The rape of male by male has more to do with primitive drives to dominate rival males than it has to do with sex. Male primates assert their dominance by mounting rival males and so seldom bother with low-ranking males who pose no threat. Most male rape victims are heterosexual, as are most of the men who rape men. Had you been perceived as gay you might not have stimulated this dominance ritual.

WHY WAS I RAPED AS WELL AS BEING ABUSED AS A CHILD?

A significant number of rape victims were sexually abused as children. There are several possible reasons for this. Abused people are often preoccupied with the problems caused by a lack of self-esteem, which means they can be less alert to danger or more compliant in dangerous situations. Low self-esteem can make it hard to resist invitations that could hold danger. There may also be collusion from the A state: 'What does it matter what happens? Life stinks anyway. It's no more than you deserve.' Meantime the V state's message may be: 'I am so awful that I am lucky to have anyone interested in me. I mustn't cross them or they'll leave me.'

Rapists often target people who are frightened and unassertive. Discovering how your self-image may have led you into danger can help keep you safe in future.

Nothing can make you even partially responsible for your own rape.

ALL SEX ORGANS DISGUST ME. WILL IT STAY THAT WAY?

Trauma associated with anything – horses, fire, enclosed spaces – can cause a phobia. Someone who has been abused may fear the instrument that was used to abuse them, yet when we really think about it a penis is intrinsically no more disgusting than a nose, a vagina no more repellent than a mouth. Your response to them is learned, you were not born with it. Genitals, like cars, are neutral; it is what people do with them that can injure. Just as people with spider phobias can be gradually desensitized, so can you.

CAN I AVOID BEING RAPED AGAIN?

This is the big question. The sad truth is that there is no cast-iron guarantee, but there are measures you can take which will reduce the chances. Here are some defensive actions.

1 *Analyse your rape carefully. Could you have done anything to avoid it? A 'yes' answer is good. If looking after yourself better could have avoided the rape, you have a good chance of staying safe.*

2 *Watch your body language. Walk purposefully, keep your head high. If you meet someone's gaze, do not drop your head. Your body language must say: 'I know where I am going, mess with me at your peril.'*

3 *If a person in a car stops to ask directions, stand back and increase the volume of your voice. In other words, keep out of reach and sound assertive.*

4 *Late at night after clubbing or a party, go home in a group or arrange a taxi in advance. Do not give or take lifts from comparative strangers.*

Shirley

After a dinner party, Margaret, Shirley's hostess, asked her to drop off another guest, Colin. Shirley, who had been raped, felt trapped by the request. To refuse would seem churlish and, as Margaret asked in front of Colin, confrontational. At first Shirley responded in her old compliant way, but then she felt the panic twist in her abdomen. Pushing herself out of her V state and into her I state, she spoke privately with Margaret. She explained that she had not wanted to embarrass her hostess by refusing the lift, but she was not prepared to take Colin alone. She did not make the mistake of rescuing Margaret from her dilemma.

When it was time to leave, Margaret said casually, 'I feel like some air after all that food. May I drive you home?' Never again did she ask Shirley to give a lift to someone she had just met. She owned that she should have consulted Shirley in private before compromising her. Both women learned a lesson in safety.

5 *If your domestic circumstances are suitable, you might consider having a dog. A dog will take over the job of listening for intruders.*

This means you no longer have to keep the sound on your TV low so that you can hear anything that may be threatening. Many criminals will admit that they will not enter premises where there is even a small dog. With a dog as protection, you can allow yourself to sleep deeply.

You are also protected with a dog on the street and in the car, provided you choose a suitable dog – sweet and cuddly is not on the shopping list. Certain breeds, such as German Shepherd dogs, carry a visual message because of their use by the police and military. This does not mean that they are aggressive, only that some have been trained to be so. You do not need an aggressive dog. You do need an adult dog, large and preferably female, as bitches are generally more protective. Probably the best place to find the dog you need is a rehoming centre such as those run by animal welfare societies. There you will find a large selection and be given time to get to know the dog.

There are also therapeutic advantages to having a loving animal in close proximity. Trust will build up between you, which is a good way to begin to learn to trust again. It has also been shown that physical contact with animals can reduce stress. Feeling safe will influence your body language and thus the subliminal messages you broadcast.

6 If living with a dog is not for you, there are other ways of feeling safe. What it is legal to carry for defensive purposes differs widely according to where you live. Your local police force or Rape Crisis centre will tell you what you may or may not carry.

7 A course in self-defence is a double whammy, as just knowing that you can defend yourself will boost your confidence and this will show in your body language (see Michelle's story opposite.)

8 Carry a screamer personal alarm.

9 If someone you do not want to have sex with is in unwanted physical contact with you, leave no room for doubt or misinterpretation. Do not try to laugh it off. Sometimes potential rapists can be shocked back to reality by clear statements such as: 'If you do not let go, this will be assault, unless you intend rape.'

10 In a sexually threatening situation it is important that the potential rapist sees you as a person. Make sure they know your name,

Michelle

Michelle, who had been raped a year previously, was passing through the Bahamas when she unknowingly booked a room in the red-light district where few tourists had been before. As she headed for her room at night she was surrounded by a group of three men who demanded her handbag. Knowing no more about kung fu than she had seen in the in-flight movie, she found herself striking what she hoped was a serious kung fu pose and claiming to be a police officer. One of the men lunged at her, tripped on the curb and fell. Michelle took out a make-up compact and 'called for backup'. The men ran away.

Michelle had not checked that her room was in a safe area, but she could take pleasure in knowing that a keenly defensive part of her — her modified A state — had manifested when she was threatened, whereas previously she had perceived herself as a victim. After this triumph she gradually began to trust the inventive part of herself which had intimidated three men into accepting her version of reality over their own. As a result of this dramatic episode she felt safer and eventually took better care of herself.

something about your children or parents or job. Keep talking aboutyourself to separate your image from the rapist's fantasy victim. If you do not play the role in which the rapist has cast you there is a chance that the script will be dumped.

11 Many people defend their right to wear the clothes they choose, however sexual the clothes' message might be and regardless of how a sick mind might interpret them. When clothes disable their wearer it might be time to compromise. The high moral ground can be a very dangerous place, so defensive clothes are a serious option. Shoes that lengthen legs rarely enhance agility; clothes which accentuate buttocks rarely give freedom of movement. It is prudent to wear flat shoes and cover sexy clothes when travelling to and from places where they are appropriate. It is hard to stare down an aroused attacker over a mound of cleavage.

12 *Because many male rapists have been abused by their parents it can be useful to talk about your own 'appalling parents' so that they identify you as a fellow sufferer and not as a symbolic abuser.*

Marcia

Marcia was working alone in her office when an agitated man pushed his way in, asking for a friend he believed worked there. He said he had left his hostel that morning and hitched several miles. He had also left his tablets at home and 'they' said he must take them.

Marcia, in one of those rare flashes of inspiration, said, 'I'm so glad you are here. I heard funny noises from the kitchen and I think someone is trying to break in.' The man, who had been showing signs of being in his A state, immediately turned his animosity for Marcia into defensiveness. He assured Marcia that she would be safe with him there and he strode into the kitchen.

Marcia thanked him and treated him as if he was her protector. After a while he agreed that she should phone a report of the intruder to the police. When the police arrived they drove him back to his hostel and his anti-psychotic drugs.

9

Healing Your Feelings

Dreams, Nightmares, Paralysis and Replays

There are many different beliefs about the purpose of dreams, and it may be that dreams have many functions, one of which is to help us express any build-up of feelings not released during waking hours. Another function may be to help us process those events which require a lot of 'digesting', such as rape and childhood sexual abuse, which would explain why horrific events sometimes take place in our brain while we sleep.

One of the most distressing sleep experiences is waking to find yourself momentarily paralysed. The explanation probably lies in the nature of sleep.

Sleep comprises a number of different stages. The one in which dreams occur is known as REM or rapid eye movement sleep. During this phase the brain produces chemicals which prevent the sleeper from physically acting out his dream. This does not always work totally, as anyone who has sleepwalked or who has a partner who thrashes around and talks in his sleep knows. Sometimes the chemical does not de-activate immediately the sleeper wakes, producing the paralysed sensation which can be so frightening. This often occurs after a sensation of being re-abused, maybe even of having an abuser lying on top of your body preventing normal breathing.

The sensation of having someone on top of us, crushing the chest, is believed to be caused by an ancient limbic device for slowing the bodily functions so that we could stay underwater for longer periods, or perhaps maximize available food during lean times, much as hibernating animals do.

Even without the paralysis, nightmares can feel more real than reality. Why would they not? We experience events in the outside world through our sensory receptors which then produce the sensations and emotions we experience in our brain. When stimulated from within, as with dreams and fantasies, the brain also produces sensations and emotions, and these can be indistinguishable from those generated by the outside world. So the phrase 'It's only a nightmare' can be disrespectful of an appalling experience which may haunt the dreamer for some time. Luckily such dreams also present a golden healing opportunity.

MAKING YOUR NIGHTMARES WORK FOR YOU

Some people like to keep a separate 'dream book' in which to write down their dreams or nightmares. Keep your book or a tape recorder by your bed and record your nightmare immediately you wake. You may think you will remember the dream later, but evidence shows that we forget large parts of our dreams.

If you are distressed, work on the dream immediately. Draw it in sequence, like a comic strip. If you dream in colour, use colours as close to those of the dream as possible. Select the most distressing parts of the dream and redraw them, changing the most horrific aspects to make them less frightening.

Jenny

Jenny dreamed she was locked in an old-fashioned lavatory. She looked in the bowl and saw a dead baby. The bowl began to fill with blood and sewage, which overflowed until the stinking mess was up to Jenny's chin. She lost sight of the dead baby, but could feel it grasping at her legs under the mess.

Jenny changed her dream. She found a piece of string floating in the mess and pulled on it. This pulled a plug in the floor and the sludge drained away. Jenny picked up the baby, which was alive, and took it into a shower she created outside the lavatory. She and the baby showered clean and Jenny gave herself a fluffy white robe and wrapped the baby in a soft white towel. The baby was wise and enchanting, and Jenny took it outside into a soft green garden where they played together in the sun.

Some dreams are long and complicated and may need breaking down into chunks. The chunks do not have to be consistent. In another part of Jenny's dream she was washed out of the lavatory and out to sea where a creature — half-man, half-penis — pursued her, cutting through waters which would neither support her nor allow her to move. She worked this section separately, giving herself four dolphins which carried her to a safe island.

Flashbacks

Flashbacks are action replays of emotional events which can be triggered by smells, words, sounds or sights. When the mind is not busy, they come into consciousness like a screen saver on a computer.

In many ways the workings of the mind and body mirror each other, the mind's response to a bad experience mimicking the body's reaction to bad meat. If the mind finds an experience difficult to process, it will keep throwing it back, undigested. Flashbacks are experiences returned to the conscious mind for processing into a form the unconscious mind can digest. It can then incorporate the experience in its data banks for use in the future, just as the body uses infections to create antibodies against future viral attacks.

The unconscious will use almost any trigger to re-run an indigestible experience. Even though this may feel threatening, it is part of an automatic healing process comparable to your body's healing process. When you have influenza, your sore throat and cough are the result of your body's defence system trying to remove the invading virus. It hurts, but it is for your protection. Just as you need to cooperate with your body, so you need to aid your mind's healing process by using your conscious mind to help digest your bad experience.

WORKING WITH FLASHBACKS

The following is a technique for working with your unconscious mind so that you can 'hear' its message.

1 *Write down in detail all that happens in your flashbacks. This may take some time, but the act of writing it down tells your unconscious that you are listening to it and respecting its healing process.*

2 *Read through what you have written and assess your distress on a scale from one to five, with a panic attack counting as five and slight discomfort as one.*

3 *For a score of one to three, record your account on tape and listen to it every day, stopping the tape when you are aware of a very strong feeling. In your book write a message of comfort to yourself as you were at that moment. For example:*

I know you can't breathe because he has his arm over your throat. The floor stinks, I know. His breath is foul and you think your shoulder may be dislocated. You're right, it is irrational to worry about wetting yourself, but who can be rational when their brain is in turmoil and they are in so much pain? You think you may vomit and you wonder if you will choke on it, but you won't. You will get away.

Continue until you have worked through the entire tape. If you are not in therapy you might care also to recount the experience to a Rape Crisis volunteer. Your objective is to be able to relive the experience without distress.

4 *For a score of three to five, record the experience again using only one of your senses, starting with the least distressing. Choose from: emotion, sound, sight, smell, taste or touch. The following example uses sound:*

I hear my voice. It is saying 'Please' over and over again. I hear his voice. He is saying, 'Lovely, lovely.' I hear the rustle of his clothes. Then there is the sound of footsteps and laughter. It is very far away. There is the sound of traffic. He is saying, 'Beg me, it won't be so bad if you beg me.'

When you have been through the entire tape, telling your story in each of your senses, listen to your original tape again and reassess your feelings.

Do not rush these exercises. They may take months. Proceed at a pace that feels safe to you and which does not violate your feelings. Do not hesitate to ask for help from the people recommended in Chapter 11. Remember, they are working in their chosen field and they want to work with you.

Practical Work

Healing Your Feelings

Q: 'How do you eat an elephant?'
A: 'A little bit at a time.'

In your book list the feelings you want to regain and the feelings you want to lose. Make separate columns so that you can mark them off as you achieve your goals.

Feelings often chosen to be jettisoned include: *anger, fear, obsession, asexuality, a sense of being unclean* and *the need for revenge.* Start with the negative feeling that is easiest to tackle.

Those to be regained can be: *sexual feelings, trust, pride in your own appearance* and *a sense of safety.*

VENT YOUR ANGER *(USING YOUR A STATE)*
When you are alone or with someone with whom you feel comfortable, find a punch bag, a bean bag or your mattress. Draw your attacker(s) and stick the drawing on your bag or mattress. Remember, this is not an art class – your unconscious can 'see' what your drawing represents. Find a piece of power music – eg Wagner's *Ride of the Valkyries* or Meatloaf's *Bat out of Hell.* Listen and move to the music for a while and then, using your fists or a weapon, attack the drawing in time to the music.

At first you may feel nothing, but persevere. Eventually you will almost certainly experience rage. Enjoy it. Victimless, and therefore guiltless, rage is a cathartic and exhilarating experience. You will feel high afterwards. Your anger and the physical exercise will have released natural chemicals, much like morphine, into your bloodstream.

You may need a therapeutic cry afterwards. Make sure you have nothing else to do for the rest of the day and cry all you like. Write an account of the experience in your book.

Repeat the exercise until the anger is only there when you want it.

HIT BACK (*USING YOUR A STATE*)

Buy a neutral-looking rag or plastic doll. Place it on your anger cushion. Make a symbolic change to the figure – if your attacker had a moustache, draw a moustache on the figure. In your mind make it your attacker. Be perfectly still and listen to your Self. What do you want to do to this person? Do it to the doll.

Remember, wanting to retaliate is healthy and natural. The feelings occur automatically in your limbic brain (*see* pages 65–6) as the result of being attacked. You can experience these feelings repeatedly, like hunger, or you can satisfy them harmlessly. Dolls do not experience pain and there is nothing criminal about attacking a doll. Simply being 'nice' will not bring about a feeling of well-being.

Clive

A miserable, huddled teenager, Clive would barely speak to me. He had been raped in a public toilet while he was drunk. In response to his shock and misery his immune system was malfunctioning. Dandruff and acne added to his despair.

'What would you like to do to them, Clive?' I asked.

He shrugged and kept his eyes on the carpet.

'Some people who have been raped, Clive, want to kill the rapist. Some just want to cut their balls off.'

He looked up at me at last. 'Yeah, but you can't, can you? All you can do is think.'

I handed him some soft red latex balls and a penknife on a tray.

'What? You want me to cut those?' He looked incredulous.

'Try it. Can't hurt.'

He snorted down his nose and shrugged. ''Sright, can't hurt.'

He screwed up the balls in his hands, tears wetted his

blemished skin. He took the knife and drove it into the rubber time and again until the balls lay in spongy fragments. He looked up at me. 'That was OK,' he said – and smiled.

RESTORE YOUR SENSE OF SAFETY
(TENDING YOUR V STATE)

Do not increase your anxiety by telling yourself that you *must* do anything. But you might like to experiment with the idea of taking a self-defence course. If the idea makes you anxious, imagine how it would be if you were not scared. See yourself in the clothes. What would your instructor be like? Would you prefer judo, kung fu or something else? What sort of venue would you be in? Who else might be there? Would it be easier to be the only student? Would you like a friend to be with you?

You may feel you cannot meet people or that the instructor would terrify you. But after a few sessions in your imagination you should be ready for reality. If you are not, then please consider seeking therapy for a while. Let someone help you over the first hurdle. The gaining of new skills and the sense of power that a self-defence course offers will help to erode your feeling of vulnerability.

DISTRACT YOURSELF FROM OBSESSIONAL THINKING

Obsessional thinking builds circuits of brain cells. They are tracks we can find difficult to escape. When you feel yourself about to do a circuit, do something else – say a poem or song backwards, count back from 1,000 in decreasing numbers from 10 (990, 981, 973, etc). You need something that takes your total attention. That way your brain can begin to dismantle the circuits that keep you obsessing.

ASEXUALITY

A lack of sexual feelings is natural in your situation. After all, if a child grabs a hot poker and is burned, that child will avoid pokers for some time. You have been hurt and your unconscious does not want you to be hurt again, so it has shut down your sexual programme.

If you were raped, you can regain your sexual responses. After adult rape it is likely that they will return in time, even if you do nothing.

Draw your body in your book, then colour in where it was hurt. If it is your rectum or vagina, draw the wounds as you visualize them and ask yourself what would heal them. Wave goodbye to common sense for the moment. Tend to your body in the theatre of your mind with whatever your imagination chooses. One woman chose tears.

Act out your healing in reality as closely as possible. Having chosen tears, for example, you could bathe yourself with sea water. Remember, the more ritual you can introduce and the more senses you involve, the deeper the healing.

Remind yourself that body cells constantly change. Already your body is renewing itself. The skin that was touched by the abuser may have been totally replaced by now.

Draw your body being tended and draw it healing.

OVERCOME YOUR FEARS

Anxiety is anticipated fear. It flourishes in a malnourished body and can create a chemically self-sustaining imbalance. Your body has been hurt, so feed it, exercise it, give it your total care. When you are anxious, assist your body to regulate itself by using the adrenalin you are pumping into your bloodstream to exercise. Do your anger exercises or dance to music with empowering lyrics. People have found the following useful: *These Boots Were Made for Walking* by Nancy Sinatra, *Punch* by Marillion, *I Will Survive* by Gloria Gaynor, Holst's 'Mars' from *The Planet Suite,* or Ravel's *Bolero.*

For Men Who Have Been Raped

MOVING SELF-BLAME

Write down all the negative things you are feeling about yourself. For example:

You will never be the same again. If you weren't such a wimp you could have prevented the rape. If anyone knew you had been raped they would laugh at you. Better not let anyone become close to you lest they find out. You feel out of control, as if your mind is a strange place full of explosives. You might do anything. You are not safe and you don't deserve to be safe.

Choose a man for whom you have affection and respect – a son, brother or father is fine. If you have a photograph of him, get a life-size enlargement of his face. If you have no photograph, draw him. (Don't worry if your drawing does not look much like him, your unconscious knows who it is.) Place the picture at eye level and stand close. Step by step imagine the person in the picture being humiliated and raped in exactly the way you were.

When you have played the memory with your substitute, read him your statement. You will find it hard to do, but finish. The more difficult it is to abuse your substitute the more deeply your emotional abuse of yourself will impact you and the easier it will be to accept help because you can believe that you deserve it.

Write a second statement to your substitute, telling him why he did not deserve what happened to him. Read it to your picture. Cry if you want to.

Creating a New Self

YOUR IDENTICAL TWIN

Imagine you have an identical twin, separated from you at birth, who had an ideal childhood, full of learning, love, respect and fun. How would this twin be? How different would this twin look? Feel? Act?

Begin to design your twin's childhood. Cut out pictures of home and of mother and father from magazines. Are there brothers? Sisters? Pets? Holidays? School triumphs? Friends? Cut out pictures that give you the feeling of family. It doesn't matter if you use several different people to show different aspects of one personality.

What would school be like? Would there be horses to ride at home? What would the family do at weekends? How would the living room be furnished? What food would be eaten? Be as detailed and elaborate as you can, and create a whole series of drawings or collages. Do not worry if you get a bit obsessive, this will pass as you heal. Make up stories about the family. Does your twin travel? What does your mother do for a living?

Here you are using false memory in a positive, healing way. You know these are not real memories, but your unconscious mind can use them as a resource. You are beginning to 'polyfill' your psyche, filling the holes in it with love and fun and happiness.

Cherish each collage. Hang it in a prominent position. Experiment with adding smells and sounds. Look at your collage while playing suitable music – if you have designed a family holiday in Greece, play Greek music. Olive oil and basil are smells evocative of Greece. Don't forget to raise the temperature of the room!

When you face a challenging situation, think yourself into being your privileged twin. You now have very little negative baggage. Dress like your twin, eat like your twin, stand like your twin. Imagine you have traded places for difficult situations.

In your healing book list the things you have to teach your twin. Do not allow your V state to get away with 'I have nothing to teach.' Start with 'I have survived trauma. My twin is still untried.'

10

For You and Your Partner

RAPE AND CSA VERY rarely have one victim. The partners of victims of assault have emotional needs which are too often drowned in the needs of the victim. Men in particular are apt to experience an irrational sense of having failed to protect their woman. Partners' homes and lives are also violated by the abuser, and the partners of rape victims may have the agony of waiting for the results of AIDS and pregnancy tests. Both heterosexual and gay partners may find themselves rejected in what was a loving relationship before the assault. Their independent fun-loving partner may become clingy, demanding and depressed.

The ultimate difficulty for any partner is not to be told of a rape and to find that he has contracted a sexually-transmitted disease as a result. This is hard to forgive, and it is equally hard to understand that the truth was probably withheld not out of deceit but as a result of shock and irrational shame. The mind accommodates shock in strange ways, one of which is to act as if nothing has happened. This is known as denial.

Some partners are consumed by the need for the revenge which is denied them. Caught in the no-go area between arousal and action, they are trapped in a restless, impotent need for satisfaction which can only be resolved by taking symbolic action.

The partners of adult assault victims sometimes feel betrayed by their partner. They know this to be irrational and blame themselves. The internal conflict between the parts of them that want to love and support (I state) and the irrational overwhelming feelings (Primitive, V state and A state) can cause them to turn away from the situation. This leaves the rape victim feeling rejected at a time when she most needs acceptance. In such circumstances it is vital that the couple receives the help of a skilled professional, someone dispassionate to ensure that communications between partners are understood. Without this it is easy for the pair to drown in a sea of misunderstanding, each hearing what they fear the other is saying.

The Male Partners of Assaulted Women

If your partner has been assaulted, you may have feelings you cannot rationalize. Of course you want to help, but perhaps you, too, are feeling emotional and confused. You may feel a great need to make love to your partner, but you may also feel angry with her or that you do not want to touch her. You may feel your own masculinity has been diminished by what has happened. Your emotional turmoil may be so great that you doubt your ability to handle it.

Your I state knows that your partner needs help and support, and your inability to give it may add guilt to the list of emotions vying for supremacy in your mind. But it is not selfish to take care of your own needs right now − ignoring them may imperil your relationship. Some men try so hard to do the right thing that they ignore their own feelings until they are overwhelmed by them. Their behaviour can then become problematic and they may be accused of abandoning their partners. Most men handle trauma by withdrawing into themselves until their mind has sorted out the problem. They can function socially, or at work, but they find it hard to talk to their nearest and dearest. Women need communication and reassurance. The bravest and most useful action is to be with your partner, if this is what she needs, but a game of squash and a few beers now and then may be essential for your own well-being.

Your anger with the rapist is natural and there is no doubt that if you were able to pulp him with no comeback you would feel a lot better. Some men feel so agitated when their partners are raped that they need to be out on the streets or with a group of other men.

You know that being angry with your partner is inappropriate and yet you may still feel anger. This may stem from the simple values of our limbic brain, which is concerned only with reproduction and survival. Some other mammals punish their mates when they have been raped. The evolutionary motive for this Primitive behaviour may be to encourage the female to put up more of a fight next time or, through stress, to lose any embryo conceived from the rape. This gives the male a better chance of ensuring that it is his genes which survive into the next generation.

You may feel a strong need to make love to your partner as soon after the rape as possible. This urge may come from more than one part of you: from your I state comes the conscious need to offer love, comfort and intimacy the way you always have, while from your Primitive stems the drive to 'wash away' the semen of a rival and thus ensure the domination of your genes. These drives may create your impulses but they need not control your behaviour. We still run partly on outdated wiring and while the forest primate does not know what dictates his impulses, you do. Your reason and love and loyalty are enough to overpower limbic dictates.

HOW TO HELP HER
Your partner may need to talk to you about what has happened to her – remember, she may have believed she was going to die – and it is good for her to talk, but only when she

is ready. There is a popular misconception that all you have to do is talk about things and they miraculously heal. Your partner may not want to talk to you about her ordeal at all. It may feel as if you are the 'clean, good' part of her life and she may therefore need to keep you and any children separate from what has happened. She may also feel that she will hurt you by talking about it and want to protect you.

If your partner does talk to you about what happened to her, you may notice that the story sometimes changes and this may cause you to doubt her in some way. Don't. Research on the nature of traumatic memory shows us that memories change as we try to process them. It is important that your partner feels free from criticism and is able to process the memories in her own time and in her own way.

You may get mixed messages. Your partner may fear that you will be repelled by her or that you will leave her. She may want to rebond sexually with you yet not be ready for an activity which will associate you with a terrible event which is still recent in her mind. Sometimes it is a while before a woman is ready for love-making after a major assault.

Resuming sex after a long break can be daunting for both of you. It is not easy to keep an erection when you fear your partner may be frightened or repelled, or when its lack may be seen as a rejection. Why not agree to begin with non-penetrative sex for a while, say a month to start with? You can hold and touch as much as feels safe and then gradually re-establish the sexual relationship you had before the rape.

When full sexual activity is resumed, your partner may have flashbacks of the rape. It can help if you make sure she is either looking at you or you are talking to her all the while you are making love. This helps to keep her focused on the present. Rarely, sexual love does not return naturally, and then a good sex therapist may be needed.

HIV

After the shock of sexual assault begins to recede one of the first thoughts is usually 'Could I have contracted HIV?' Ideally this question should be answered immediately. Cruelly, it cannot be answered for three long months, during which the raped person has to regard himself as a potential risk to his partner. This is especially destructive to couples who wish to make love as part of a declaration of dedication and support. The need to use a condom can make it seem as if the rapist has literally separated the couple.

Should the HIV test be positive, it is as if the rapist has not only violated but may have murdered. The victim should have skilled help available, for although he may never develop AIDS, he has to live with this possibility, as well as the restrictions of being HIV positive. Whilst it is not possible to know immediately whether the HIV has been contracted from the abuser, many assaulted people are asked to have an AIDS test soon after the attack to help clarify whether the virus was caught from the assailant or was already present.

Children's bodies are especially vulnerable to tearing, which makes it easy for the HIV virus to invade the body.

Pregnant Rape Victims

The pregnant rape victim who contracts HIV from her rapist may well struggle with the decision of whether or not to terminate her pregnancy – an agonizing decision that has to be taken at a time when the victim is perhaps least able to make it.

It is the victim and her partner who will bear the consequences of the decision, so it is vital that they are not influenced by the views of others. However much they care, the most that others can do is to allow the couple to talk, knowing that talking will help them to sort out their feelings. They can also make it clear that they will support the couple's final decision, whether it reflects their own personal belief system or not. If the couple decide to terminate the pregnancy, they may feel that their bereavement has gone unrecognized and they may need the support of others.

A non-partisan professional can be of great value in helping to clarify thoughts. Of course, those who strongly believe that all abortion is wrong have less of a moral struggle, as do those who passionately believe that bearing children who are likely to suffer is morally wrong.

PREGNANT BY THE RAPIST

A woman who finds herself pregnant by her rapist has momentous decisions to make. Some women feel clearly that they want no part of the rapist in their body and are impatient to abort his embryo. Once this is done some feel able to begin the task of healing, while others experience the sense of bereavement that often follows an abortion. Grief, combined with the aftermath of rape, can lead to clinical depression.

Some women feel attached to the forming child, considering it to be part of themselves as well as the rapist; however they may fear that if they keep the child they might see the rapist in its face and behaviour. They might consider adoption as an alternative, but wonder if they will be able to bear to part with the child when the time comes.

Some women wonder about the child's genetic heritage, fearing the rapist may be mentally ill with a condition that might be passed on to his child. This fear may be particularly acute when the rapist has not been caught or identified. The woman may not even know what he looks like, his age, race or history.

A partner may be in the agonizing position of not wanting to pressurize the woman into giving up her child when she is distressed, but at the same time he may be unsure of his ability to love the child of the man who raped his partner. A partner who is unwilling to raise a rapist's child as his own may attempt to influence the woman's decision, whereas a man with powerful religious beliefs may share his wife's dilemma. He will need help for himself if he is to support his wife in continuing with her pregnancy and in making decisions about the child's future.

Couples who decide to terminate the pregnancy need support in avoiding clinical depression. Like any termination, it will cause a chemical imbalance in the body and a woman traumatized by rape is especially vulnerable. She is also vulnerable to depression following the adoption of the child, even though she may have made the right choice for herself and her family.

The Rape of Men by Men

The rape of a man by another man or men frequently involves violence. Initially the violence may be used to subdue the victim, after which it may enhance the pleasure of the rapist(s) by feeding the primitive need to dominate other males.

When the ordeal is over the victim often feels ashamed of having been raped and of not being able to defend himself. His rationality is suspended by the devastating impact of his ordeal. He may feel the need to hide what has happened and so reporting his humiliation to what he imagines will be grinning policemen is unthinkable. In the past he may have made just the kind of joke he now fears will be made about him.

Perhaps the man ejaculated during his rape and this has caused him to doubt his sexual orientation. However, few men realize that the sexual response in the male is less to do with choice than biology. Fear itself can cause erection and ejaculation.

If a man feels it necessary to keep his rape a secret, he can still work through it by seeking the help of a professional counsellor or psychotherapist. This removes the fear of others knowing. Later, when he is feeling better, he can still exercise his choice of whom, if anyone, to tell. Some men choose to report their rape anonymously so that the police are alerted to the existence and pattern of the rapist. Some brave men have allowed the police to prosecute.

Homophobia and prejudice may cause a male rape victim to fear that if he reports the rape he will be suspected of being gay. Yet all reports help to erode the idea that rape of heterosexual men is very rare.

It can seem as if the respect of the victim's family, friends and colleagues is dependent upon the rape remaining secret and so he believes he must behave as if nothing has happened. This is not ultimately helpful because eventually the emotional impact is likely to dictate behaviour. Violence, excessive drinking and risk-taking are all common ways in which a male rape victim demonstrates his feelings. Any relationship he has may break up as he withdraws deeper into himself and struggles not to show any signs of 'weakness'. Friends, not knowing what has happened to him, often withdraw as he becomes excessively competitive, needing to win every game and every argument. Job loss can follow. Male rape victims often break the law.

T E Lawrence of Arabia was reputedly raped by his Turkish captors. After this he became more violent, experienced the need for physical punishment and sank into tormented oblivion. How different things might have been had he had help to understand his reaction. Lawrence was one of millions of men who have been raped by heterosexual men as a rite of dominance.

Men normally find it difficult to talk about intimate feelings with other men, a tendency which helps to isolate male rape victims even further. As one man put it angrily: 'What do you expect me to do? Walk in the boozer, say, "Pints all round, I've just been buggered"? They're not going to come and put their bloody arms round me.'

David

David was a young-looking 19-year-old travelling through Africa gathering material for his thesis. Against advice he crossed into a country which was on the verge of civil war and where there was growing unrest and violence in the streets. He sought shelter in a cheap hotel. Suddenly, in the small hours of the morning, the flimsy door to his room was broken down by four men drunk with alcohol and power. They robbed David and then raped him for over an hour. He expected to be killed, but the men left him alive. A few days later his embassy flew him out of what had become a war zone. In the protracted war that followed, thousands were raped and slaughtered.

David had no hope of prosecuting the men who robbed and raped him. In fact he told no one. He was ashamed and blamed himself for crossing the border in the first place. He later found he was HIV positive.

The Partner of a Raped Man

The rape victim may be hostile towards his partner because he feels he has lost his masculinity and, somewhere in his mind, he believes his partner feels that too. He may become dominating or spend much of his time away in macho pursuits. He may rebuff any attempts to help, leaving his partner feeling shut out and rejected. He may make the person closest to him the butt of his anger. He might become over-protective of his children, especially boys.

If your partner has been raped and his behaviour changes towards you, you may feel angry with him and be easily provoked into outbursts of anger which leave you exhausted and feeling guilty. There is a possibility that he is unconsciously manipulating you into saying the things he secretly feels about himself. This way he hears criticism from outside himself where it is easier to face. He can remain in his Victim state while you are placed in the role of Aggressor. This can become a vicious circle, especially if he is so wounded that he is unable to work.

Your partner may not tell you about the rape until some time after it happens. You may feel betrayed by this, as if he does not trust you. Remember he is acting from shame and shock, not rationality.

DIFFICULT SECRET FEELINGS

Your own feelings about your partner may be a source of confusion. You may feel guilty because after a while you secretly feel that your partner has lost his masculinity, especially if he is depressed and out of work. You might find it difficult to desire him sexually. He may not be making love to you at all and, despite your compassion and insight, you find yourself feeling rejected and perhaps being responsive towards other men. Your sexual needs are not being met, nor are your emotional needs, and so your body will send you signals that it wants its needs satisfied. You may also feel that your sexuality is compromised by your partner's attitude. If you have been used to being the object of his desire and are so no longer, it is easy to feel uncertain of how to relate to him.

A woman's Primitive is simply trying to secure a mate who will protect and fertilize her. Your advantage is that you have centuries of experience in your unconscious that are not available to your Primitive. Furthermore, you have knowledge and understanding, so you can win this one without making your Primitive feel guilty for her genetic drives.

INFIDELITY

What if your Primitive should win and you are unfaithful? There are two major possible reactions and many stages between:

1 *You feel loathsome and guilty, almost as if you had been raped yourself.*

2 *It was wonderful and you want more.*

Neither reaction is likely to survive for long and both indicate that your relationship now needs outside professional help. You have run out of time for putting your partner's needs first and suppressing your own, because his needs and yours have become the same – he needs support; you need support. He could probably not cope with knowing of your infidelity and yet you need to tell someone, to be heard while you explore the feelings that led to your action. Most of all you need to share the weight and responsibility of the situation that has been forced on you. You have also become a victim of his rape and deserve all the outside help you can get. The alternative may well be the loss of your relationship.

HOW TO HELP HIM

Avoid becoming over-nurturing. It is tempting to take over the role your partner seems to have abandoned by becoming the sole breadwinner while he takes over the child-rearing and housework. This risks placing him in the position he most dreads yet seems to seek. Do not accept his aggression. He is having a very hard time controlling it; do not make it harder by pretending it is tolerable to you.

In some cases people have helped their assaulted partner greatly by showing that they still see him as a sexual creature, masculine and desirable. Men sometimes reject sexual activity after a rape for fear of triggering rape memories; however, sex with his partner will be so different from his rape that it is unlikely to do this. Touching and cuddling can be very reassuring for both of you. Penetrative sex can wait and it is vital not to demand it if it seems difficult for him – there is a fine line between showing that you desire him and seeming to be a sexual threat.

A couple of months after the rape is a good time to take a vacation, especially an activity holiday, where you can both meet new people and new challenges.

The Partners of Those Abused as Children

If your partner was abused as a child, he is likely to be creative, moody and emotional, and switch from one personality part to another with astounding rapidity. In one person you may well have an innovator, a dictator, a sad person in constant need of reassurance, a playful child, and so on. Your partner may berate you one moment and beg for your love the next.

Gruelling emotional scenes can leave you drained and incapable of supplying the reassurance your partner craves.

Mostly the happy, funny, inventive person will keep you in the relationship, but the sad, desperate, needy person can erode your loyalty. It is essential that you do not play the role of comforter or villain but remain in your I state so that you can explain to your partner what they are doing as it is happening, for instance: 'I don't think being 15 minutes late warrants the way you are attacking me. I am not the person you are describing.'

It is essential that the adult who was hurt so badly as a child learns to recognize that minor hurts in the present trigger huge emotions from the past, and that only the victim can address these. Once you participate in scenes which are disproportionate to their cause you rob your partner of the chance to process and grow from them. Refusing to act out the scenes should not be seen as rejection. You might say something like, 'I love you, and I know that you hurt like hell right now. I did not do this to you. Go and work in your book and I will be here when you are ready to talk to *me*, not your *father* [or uncle, etc], about my lateness.' John wrote 'Not my Shit' on an old T-shirt, which he would put on whenever his partner became irrational.

Remember, your partner's feelings are real; it is only the trigger which is bogus. Sometimes it really could be you who is at fault – we all do unkind things from time to time – and admitting your own faults can make it much easier for him to do the same. It also avoids those appalling contests in which we have to be the one who is right, whatever the reality.

Abused children rarely feel lovable and, however often love is expressed to them as adults, they cannot hold it. It slips away like soup through a patient with dysentery. Simply giving them more and more food is not the solution – first you have to cure the dysentery. If your partner assesses the relationship himself and answers his own questions, he will learn to hold love through practice, not by having it immediately replaced by more of the same. This is tough love in action.

Do not underestimate your abused partner. He will be tough in his own way, and resourceful, and if he is determined to heal, he will. He will be more used to huge emotions than you are and provided these feelings are expressed to the person who has caused them, they are healing and not dangerous.

11

Finding Support and Therapy

THIS CHAPTER IS a guide to where to go to find support and therapy, and free or inexpensive help. There is no reason why you should limit yourself to one source of support – you could use a Rape Crisis centre, the Samaritans and a therapist. It is counter-productive to have more than one therapist, but you could enlist the support of both a therapist and a psychiatrist, if they agree, especially if you are in need of psycho-active medication.

Free or Inexpensive Help and Support

SUICIDE PREVENTION AGENCIES

Groups of volunteers, such as the Samaritans, receive an enviable training and their caring listening can see you through many crises. They will not advise or treat you, but be with you on the phone or in their centre while you explore and express your feelings. They are a phone call away during those frightening, sleepless nights when fears grow like shadows behind a candle. They will not judge, nor will they demand your name, if you wish to be anonymous.

RAPE CRISIS CENTRES

Although these centres are predominantly for women, some also see men and a few are run by men for men. They vary vastly in what they offer. Some are open for a few hours a week while others operate throughout the day. Mostly the volunteers who run them are trained in the law regarding rape and in its aftermath. Most groups have the trust of the police, who will call upon them to be with you immediately after the rape if that is what you want. Often the volunteer is able to stay throughout the police and medical procedures. Usually the volunteers will continue their support right through the court case, if there is one, and beyond into reintegration into life. Some also work with partners, parents or children (secondary victims) who are traumatized by the rape.

If you decide not to go to the police, you can contact a Rape Crisis centre directly and be supported without being pressurized into reporting the rape. Like any collection of independent organizations, Rape Crisis centres differ in their philosophy and practice. Some are extreme in their feminism, which can be uncomfortable for women who do not share their views. As with all services, if you are not satisfied, say why. If things do not change, find another group which is better suited to you. Even if it is too far to travel to a centre, you can always talk on the phone.

Many Rape Crisis centres are just as concerned with adults who have been sexually abused as children and will give time and care to someone whose original trauma is many years in the past.

COLLEGE COUNSELLORS

Some colleges offer a free counselling service, so it can be worthwhile enrolling on an interesting adult learning class. An introductory counselling or psychology course would be fruitful, as what you learn can provide you with insights into your Self. It would also provide you with a peer group upon whom you can practise new ways of relating.

STUDENT COUNSELLORS

Some schools of psychotherapy and counselling offer reduced fees to those who are prepared to work with their final-year students. The work is usually of a high standard and is supervised by experts.

EMPLOYEE ASSISTANCE PROGRAMMES

It is worth checking to see whether your employer subscribes to an employee assistance programme. This is a form of insurance which covers employees for a specified number of counselling sessions, usually five. Counsellors are employed and paid by the EAP and the sessions are confidential – your employer will not learn the contents of your sessions from the agency. Some programmes will see family members.

THE POLICE

Many major stations now have special rape and sexual abuse units which consist of staff who have been specially selected for their ability to empathize with and assist those in distress. The officers receive specialized training to a high standard.

These units investigate and sometimes prosecute in child abuse cases, even when the abuse occurred many years in the past. Many also have special rape facilities designed to minimalize the unpleasantness of the necessary medical examination.

It would be unrealistic to claim that all individual officers and units are now sensitive and aware, but the culture is changing rapidly and service users contribute to these improvements by publishing their praise and complaints.

Professional Help

Choosing a professional to work with is as specialized as choosing a coat – just any old one will not do. You need to know that the branch of therapy is suitable for the job. Remember that you are the employer, so interview your potential therapist. You need to ask about specialized training and experience in this subject: rape needs to be treated by a therapist trained in working with post-traumatic shock syndrome; for CSA it is helpful if the therapist has had specialist experience and/or training.

There should also be a rapport between you and your therapist, for this relationship is like no other, and yet, paradoxically, it incorporates elements of all your vital relationships: your therapist is your mentor, your guide, your mirror, your support and your confidant(e). But your therapist remains detached from your life; they are not your friend in the sense of sharing confidences, or being there for each other. For therapy to work, you must live separate lives. It is a relationship which is close yet distant.

COUNSELLORS AND PSYCHOTHERAPISTS
These professions work largely with words, listening, challenging old beliefs and assisting the client to face and express emotions which are out of awareness and yet control from the shadows of the mind.

PSYCHOANALYSIS
This is a very long and expensive process. It can take many years and is not suitable for healing sexual trauma.

PSYCHIATRISTS
Unlike other therapists, psychiatrists are permitted to prescribe medicines. They have specialist knowledge of medications to combat depression, anxiety and delusional states. There is no doubt that some are exceptional therapists. As with other therapists, you need to choose one who has specialist knowledge of sexual abuse.

PSYCHOLOGISTS
The training received by psychologists provides an excellent background for further studies, but will not in itself equip

someone to work therapeutically. For this a clinical psychologist is necessary. As with the other professionals, a specific training or study of sexual abuse is highly desirable.

HYPNOTHERAPY

You may well see advertising material which suggests that hypnotherapy can cure you of all your pain in a few hours. This is seductive – who would not want it? The truth is that hypnosis is a very useful tool in the hands of someone well trained in matters of the mind. It is a tool to be used with discretion and expertise and when it is it can be a useful part, but only a part, of healing the wounds of CSA. If you are severely traumatized, it is better to work with a therapist who has counselling or psychotherapy qualifications in addition to their training in hypnosis. Hypnotherapy is unregulated in many countries, so please take the precaution of checking up on the practitioner's qualifications.

PSYCHODYNAMIC TECHNIQUE

This relies upon powerful childhood relationships being re-experienced with the counsellor and resolved. Pure psychodynamism requires the therapist to be a 'blank screen' in order for the childhood feelings to manifest. Many therapists with a psychodynamic background are prepared to work differently with sexual trauma. Psychodynamism is a thorough way of working and useful for those who have resolved the effects of early sexual abuse. It is not suitable for new rape trauma.

HUMANISTIC APPROACHES

These offer a more open and equal relationship between client and therapist and include a smorgasbord of techniques which can be matched to the client's needs.

'FAST CURES' FOR CSA

Beware of practitioners who offer 'fast cure' therapies for CSA, such as cult-like programmes, or a couple of weeks or hours of 'miracle therapy'. People are not formulas and need to work at their own pace. It takes time and effort to cure a lifetime of distorted self-belief and self-destructive behaviour patterns. There is also a danger, having invested considerable sums of money, of the client feeling they must be compliant in order to benefit. When they do not feel 'cured' they fall back on the old mechanisms, blaming themselves or pretending to be better to avoid conflict, and are in danger of feeling they are 'incurable' or that they have failed once again.

In Therapy

Stick with your therapist once you have made your choice, except in the unlikely event of a breach of professional ethics. If you are recovering from CSA there may be times when you feel hopelessly dependent. However unlikely it may seem at the beginning of therapy, you may feel a deep affection and erotic attraction to your therapist that is so powerful that you long for an unprofessional relationship. It is by *not* having such a relationship that you will heal.

No competent professional will have a sexual relation-ship with a client. The therapist is in the symbolic position of parent, and a good parent does not violate a child. Instead the therapist encourages the client to understand her feelings in order to be in control of her actions. A good therapist feels privileged by the affection and helps the client to learn that she can engender respect and affection without sex.

CONFIDENTIALITY
The only time confidentiality should be broken – and then only after discussion with you – is if the counsellor believes you are likely to harm yourself or another person.

What Next?

Taking Your New Self Out

When you have worked through the exercises and filled a few books, designed some procedures for yourself, read some more books, littered the mantelpiece with models of your personality parts, used yards of audiotape and the felt-tips are dry, you are likely to be feeling quite different.

You probably look different too: perhaps your hair is styled differently and your skin and body are showing the benefit of reduced stress. You have extra energy now that you are not abusing yourself or combating shock symptoms.

You may notice that strangers react to you more warmly. Your family may be less tense around you. This is the time to fight the urge to keep friends who relate to you from the 'ain't it awful' position, or who use you, or have coping mechanisms such as excessive alcohol, however much you may have relied on these friends in the past.

Avoid thinking that because you have changed you are therefore ready to heal others. If you were a jelly, you would have just been poured into the mould. You are not set yet. Everything is there, but you need the environment to make you solid.

If you were a sexually abused child, or have suffered for a long time from the effects of your rape, you probably need safe places to take your new Self, especially if you have never had a group of healthy friends. Take classes in something you know nothing about. Maybe try out a new physical activity such as skating, judo, sailing or riding. All of these activities will place you in a group of people who are exhilarated by what they are doing at the same time as you are – remember the chemist in your brain – and from this state friendships grow.

Continue to mark your progress. Growth does not have to stop.

Practical Work

Each month tape record a message to the person you will be in one year's time. Tell your future Self how you are feeling now and what you want from the 'you' in the future. Setting up an expectation of your future Self in this way helps your unconscious mind to work on what you want from the future.

It is astounding how easily we forget the way we were even one year previously. Also 'mind-editing' can deny us the chance of realizing how much we have achieved. You may be surprised at how much you look forward to your monthly tape in a year's time.

Further Reading

CHILD SEXUAL ABUSE
Peter Dale, *Adults Abused as Children,* Sage, 1999
David Finkelhor, *Sourcebook on Child Sexual Abuse,* Sage, 1986
Robin Fox, *The Red Lamp of Incest,* Hutchinson,1984
J M Masson, *The Assault on Truth,* Penguin, 1998
Alice Miller, *Thou Shalt Not Be Aware,* Pluto Press, 1998
Florence Rush, *The Best Kept Secret,* McGraw Hill

THE MIND
Helen Fisher, *The Sex Contract,* Paladin
Morton Hunt, *The Universe Within,* Corgi, 1983
Jay Ingram, *The Burning House,* Penguin

MOVING ON
Eric Berne, *What Do You Say After You Say Hello?,* Corgi
Manuel J Smith, *Kicking the Fear Habit,* Bantam

Useful Addresses

RAPE AND SEXUAL ABUSE
Australia
Adelaide Tel: 08 226 8777
Brisbane Tel: 07 226 8777

Canada
Edmonton Tel: 403 423 4120
Toronto Tel: 416 597 8808

South Africa
Rape Crisis
Tel: 021 447 9762
Fax: 021 447 5458

POWA (People Opposing Women Abuse)
Tel: 011 642 4345
Fax: 011 484 3195

Lifeline
Tel: 011 781 2337
Fax: 011 781 2715

UK
The Rape Crisis Federation (England and Wales)
7 Mansfield Road, Nottingham NG1 3FB
Tel: 0115 934 8474

Edinburgh Rape Crisis
PO Box 120
Brunswick Road, Edinburgh EH3 5XX
Tel: 0131 556 9437

Rape Crisis Northern Ireland
29 Donegall Street, Belfast
Tel: 028 9032 1830

Drug Rape UK
Roofie Foundation Helpline 0800 783 2980

USA
Atlanta Tel: 404 616 4861
Chicago Tel: 312 372 4105
Dallas Tel: 214 653 8740
Denver Tel: 303 322 7273
Los Angeles Tel: 213 612 1102
New York Tel: 718 562 3755
Seattle Tel: 206 632 7273

Kidnap USA
National Center for Missing and Exploited Children
201 Wilson Boulevard, Arlington, VA 22201 3077
Tel: 703 235 3900

Rape, Abuse, and Incest National Network (RAINN)
Tel: 1-800-656-HOPE (Hotline)
www.rainn.org

FINDING THE RIGHT THERAPIST
Australia
The Australian Institute of Professional Counsellors
PO Box 260
Lutwyche, QLD 4030
Tel: 07 3857 2277

Canada
The Canadian Guidance and Counselling Association
00 220 Laurier Ave West, Ottawa, Ontario KIP 5Z9
Tel: 613 230 4236

Ireland
The Irish Association for Counselling and Therapy
8 Cumberland Street, Dun Laoghaire, Co. Dublin
Tel: 01230 0061

New Zealand
The New Zealand Association of Counsellors
17 Corokia Place, Manukau City, Auckland
Tel: 09 267 5973

UK
The Association of Professional Therapists
Katepwa House
Ashfield Park Avenue, Ross on Wye HR9 5AX
Tel: 01989 567 676

The British Association for Counselling
1 Regent's Place, Rugby CV21 2PJ
Tel: 01788 550899

USA
IAC
169 Ruffner Hall
University of Virginia, Charlottesville VA 22903
Tel: 804 924 3119

Index